# A MAN, A WOMAN AND A HIPPOPOTAMUS

**Selima Hill** grew up in a family of painters on farms in England and Wales, and has lived by the sea in Dorset for over 40 years. She was awarded The King's Gold Medal for Poetry, 2022, with special recognition for *Gloria: Selected Poems* (Bloodaxe Books, 2008). She received a Cholmondeley Award in 1986, and was a Royal Literary Fund Fellow at Exeter University in 2003-06.

She won first prize in the Arvon/*Observer* International Poetry Competition with part of *The Accumulation of Small Acts of Kindness* (1989), one of several extended sequences in *Gloria* (2008). *Gloria* also includes work from *Saying Hello at the Station* (1984), *My Darling Camel* (1988), *A Little Book of Meat* (1993), *Aeroplanes of the World* (1994), *Violet* (1997), *Bunny* (2001), *Portrait of My Lover as a Horse* (2002), *Lou-Lou* (2004) and *Red Roses* (2006).

Her later collections from Bloodaxe are: *The Hat* (2008); *Fruitcake* (2009); *People Who Like Meatballs* (2012), shortlisted for both the Forward Poetry Prize and the Costa Poetry Award; *The Sparkling Jewel of Naturism* (2014); *Jutland* (2015), shortlisted for both the T.S. Eliot Prize and the Roehampton Poetry Prize; *The Magnitude of My Sublime Existence* (2016), shortlisted for the Roehampton Poetry Prize; *Splash Like Jesus* (2017); *I May Be Stupid But I'm Not That Stupid* (2019); *Men Who Feed Pigeons* (2021), shortlisted for the 2021 T.S. Eliot Prize and 2021 Forward Prize and for the 2022 Rathbones Folio Prize; *Women in Comfortable Shoes* (2023), a Poetry Book Society Recommendation; and *A Man, a Woman & a Hippopotamus* (2025).

*Violet* was a Poetry Book Society Choice and was shortlisted for all three of the UK's major poetry prizes, the Forward Prize, T.S. Eliot Prize and Whitbread Poetry Award. *Bunny* won the Whitbread Poetry Award, was a Poetry Book Society Choice, and was shortlisted for the T.S. Eliot Prize. *Lou-Lou, The Hat* and *Women in Comfortable Shoes* were all Poetry Book Society Recommendations, while *Jutland* was a Special Commendation.

# A MAN, A WOMAN & A HIPPOPOTAMUS

SELIMA HILL

BLOODAXE BOOKS

ISBN: 978 1 78037 752 0

First published 2025 by
Bloodaxe Books Ltd,
Eastburn,
South Park,
Hexham,
Northumberland NE46 1BS.

**www.bloodaxebooks.com**
For further information about Bloodaxe titles
please visit our website and join our mailing list
or write to the above address for a catalogue.

Cover design: Neil Astley & Pamela Robertson-Pearce.

Printed in Great Britain by Bell & Bain Limited, 303 Burnfield Road, Thornliebank, Glasgow G46 7UQ, Scotland, on acid-free paper sourced from mills with FSC chain of custody certification.

# CONTENTS

SELF-PORTRAIT WITH A BUCKET
28 Self-portrait with an Armadillo
28 Self-portrait on a Bathmat
28 Self-portrait with a Beautiful Face
29 Self-portrait with the Blessed Virgin Mary
29 Self-portrait with a Book
29 Self-portrait with My Brother
30 Self-portrait with a Bunch of Roses in Front of My Face
30 Self-portrait as a Corpse
30 Self-portrait with a Cowpat
31 Self-portrait with Crawling Mothers
31 Self-portrait with a Crown of Thorns
31 Self-portrait in a Cupboard
32 Self-portrait with Curly Hair, Holding a Mushroom
32 Self-portrait as Their Daughter
33 Self-portrait, Deep in Thought
33 Self-portrait with a Doe
33 Self-portrait as a Duck
34 Self-portrait as a Footballer, Carrying a Bucket
34 Self-portrait with a Furious Headmaster
34 Self-portrait in Goggles
35 Self-portrait with a Hammer
35 Self-portrait with a Hornet
35 Self-portrait with My Husband
36 Self-portrait with a Jelly on My Head
36 Self-portrait in a Jumbo Jet
36 Self-portrait in the Kitchen with a Spoon
37 Self-portrait with a Lettuce
37 Self-portrait in the Lido
37 Self-portrait with a Mosquito
38 Self-portrait with My Mother-in-Law
38 Self-portrait as Myself
38 Self-portrait with a Neighbour Who Doesn't Like Swimming

39 Self-portrait in 1975
39 Self-portrait with Novak Djokovik
39 Self-portrait in a Pair of Expensive Italian High Heels
40 Self-portrait with a Pair of Tweezers
40 Self-portrait with a Pan of Tomato Sauce
40 Self-portrait with a Parrot on My Shoulder
41 Self-portrait with Parsley
41 Self-portrait in a Peach-coloured Bath
41 Self-portrait as a Pebble
42 Self-portrait with a Piglet
42 Self-portrait as a Pilot
42 Self-portrait with a Pound of Flesh
43 Self-portrait in a Restaurant
43 Self-portrait in a Sauna
43 Self-portrait at the Seaside
44 Self-portrait in Several Harnesses
44 Self-portrait with a Shoe
44 Self-portrait in the Shower
45 Self-portrait in a Side Room
45 Self-portrait as a Sock
45 Self-portrait Standing in a Queue Beside a Businessman
46 Self-portrait with Straightened Hair
46 Self-portrait with a Tin of Golden Syrup
46 Self-portrait with the Toenail of a Saint
47 Self-portrait as a Tufty-eared Red River Hog
47 Self-portrait with an Umbrella
47 Self-portrait, Undressed
48 Self-portrait with an Unknown Man
48 Self-portrait with a Wall
48 Self-portrait with X in the Dark Woods

THE MATHEMATICIAN
50 Classic Cars
50 The Cake
50 Bear
51 Having to Remember Every Day

51 The Picnic
52 Far into the Night
52 Friends
52 Violins and Salad
53 The Mathematician and the Parrot
53 Friendship
53 The Value of Difficult People
54 What He Likes About His New Home
54 Sunshine
55 Eels
55 The Meeting
55 Buns
55 The Man on the Sofa (1)
56 Bananas
56 Dogs and Bears
56 The Angry Man
56 Girls Like Me
57 Doing Something Drastic About My Hair
58 The Emperor
58 Vermiculite (1)
58 And Another Question
59 The Man on the Sofa (2)
59 The Fence
59 The Colour of the Cushion
60 The Upside-down Dog
60 The Graceless Man
60 The Yellow Lorry
61 The Driver
61 The Anniversary
61 The Visitors
62 The Nursery
62 The Meaning of Barf
62 The Clap of Thunder
62 Persian Primer
63 Helping Others
63 My Friend in the Woolly Hat

63 The Nose
64 The Bear Woman
64 Dogs and Mathematicians
64 Vermiculite (2)
65 Bras in the Sun
65 The Whistling Man
65 Sunday Afternoon
66 Violence
66 Sleep
66 What I'm Trying to Say

A MAN, A WOMAN AND A CHIHUAHUA
68 A Man, A Woman and a Crossword Puzzle
68 A Man, A Woman and A Piece of Cake
68 A New Pair of Boots
68 Annabel
68 Bring Nadine
69 But People Do Love You
69 Can I Get You Something?
69 Cooked Breakfasts and Shrieks
69 Dead Flies
70 Dinner with My Father
70 Eggs
70 Expensive Cheeses
70 Field Guide to Spiders of Britain and Northern Europe
71 Friendly People
71 He's Got More Money Than He Knows What To Do With
71 His Ebullient Aunt's Latest Adventures in Eastern Europe and the Third World
71 His Little Sausage
71 Home
72 Ice Cream and Jelly
72 Impatience
72 It Hasn't Stopped Raining for Days
72 J.
73 Mary

73 Midnight
73 My Bony Hands
73 My Miserable Sister
73 'My Miserable Sister'
74 Nudity
74 Panther
74 Peaburgers
74 PRIVATE
75 Roly
75 Sardines
75 Sex with Jockeys
75 Sheep
75 Sin
76 Swimming with the Banker
76 The Afternoon of Her Arrival
76 The Air in the Mountains
76 The Answer Is Yes
76 The Box of Chocolates
77 The Chocolate Chip Cookie That My Daughter Had Given Me
77 The Ear
77 The Empty Room
77 The Ewe
78 The Famous Museum
78 The Fox
78 The Funeral
78 The Gift
79 The Hare
79 The Heart-throb
79 The Holiday-makers
79 The Key
79 The Little Dog
80 The Lonely Son
80 The Long Boring Journey
80 The Loony-bin
80 The Man in the Ugly Shoes

81 The Man Next Door
81 The Man with Four Dogs
81 The Mental Health of Footballers
81 The Orange Towel
82 The Perfect Coat
82 The Picture of His Mother
82 The Resident
82 The Sculpture
83 The Singer
83 The Sobbing Woman Lying on the Floor
83 The Spider
83 The Swimmer and the Man in a Tweed Coat
84 The Visitor
84 The Woman by the River
84 The Woman Who Doesn't Smile
84 Two Things I Know about the Hummingbird Hawk-moth
84 Two Women I Don't Recognise
85 Two Women in a Restaurant
85 Uncles
85 Vodka
85 Wednesday Afternoon at the Lido
85 Welcome Home
86 What Makes Me Happy

BABY PETER

88 The Tent
88 Pig
89 Woman Alone in a Flat
90 Strawberry Jam
91 The Waltzer
91 Cuckoo
92 Baby Peter and the Cushions
92 From His Bedroom on the Fourteenth Floor
93 A Good Boy
93 The Verger's Toes
94 Baby Peter and the Rats

94 Miserable Owls
95 Baby Peter and the Good Shepherd
95 Children in Go-karts
96 The Reservoir
96 Baby Peter Lying on the Mat
97 Catalogues
97 The Fight in the Snow
98 Orange Squash
98 The Accident
99 Beetle Mother
99 To Be the Mother of a Helpless Baby
99 Brothers for Peter
100 Pity
100 Pork
100 Baby Peter's Orange Bear
101 Baby Peter and the Doll
101 No One Ever Tells You
102 Cake
102 Yellow Grass

**AGATHA**

104 The Billionaire in His Office
104 Yachts at Sea
105 In the Silence of the Hush
105 Intimacy
106 How Old is Old?
106 Whippets
106 Sunday Nights at the Care Home
107 Sadness
107 Soup
107 Old People in Tea-rooms
108 The Happy Faces of the Very Old
108 The Young
108 The Simple Fact
109 White Mice
109 Chocolate Biscuits

109 Sleepless Nights
110 The Horse
110 Like the Lost at Sea
110 The Petite Housewife
111 The Ewe
111 Chocolate-tipped Meringues
112 Rich and Famous
112 The Residents
113 George
113 The Billionairess
113 Skin
114 Smile, Smile, Smile
114 Woman in a Chair
115 The Tablecloth
115 The Elderly
116 Concrete in May
116 Ugly Shoes
116 Happy Little Faces
117 Does He Want to Reach a Ripe Old Age?
117 Men in Winter
117 Meeting the Vicar
118 Wilhelmina
118 Pool
119 The Old Exist
119 What They Still Remember
119 Being Old is Such a Waste of Time
120 Duck
120 Cooking
121 Spectacles
121 The Old Woman and the Young Man
121 People Who Are Old Don't Have Fun
122 These Furious Adults
122 He Died the Way He Chose to Die
122 People Who Are Old Are No Fun
123 Mothers
123 The Warm Hot-water-bottle

124 What's the Point of Being Happy?
124 People Who Are Old Can't Be Trusted
124 Brassieres
125 The Father of the Late Billionaire
125 Success
125 Debut Novels
126 You Can Ask for Anything You Want
126 Mowing the Lawn
126 Spiders
127 Old Ladies
127 The Old Man and His Dog
128 Awe
128 Being Trampled on by Labradors
128 The Woman Who Escaped
129 Arthur
129 The Avenue
129 The Man Who Loved His Poodle
130 Mrs X
130 Josephine
130 Out Beyond the Cedars in their Wheelchairs

**ROOM 17**

133 The Grandmother Goes Shopping
133 A Grandmother Who Star-jumps
133 The Grandmother Goes Swimming
134 The Grandmother and Her Granddaughters
134 The Grandmother in the Park
134 The Grandmother and Coco
135 The Grandmother and Michelle at the Swimming Pool
135 The Grandmother and Her Chocolates
135 The Grandmother and the Rabbits
136 The Grandmother and the Woman Next Door
136 Grandmothers with Sweets
136 The Grandmother Relaxes
137 Grandmothers and Love
137 The Grandmother and the Visitor

137 The Grandmother and the Chickens
138 The Grandmother and the Vertiginous Hillside
138 The Grandmother and Her Carnations
138 The Grandmother and Mr Tsitsipas
139 The Grandmother in the Afternoon
139 The Grandmother and the Lion
139 The Grandmother in the Lake
140 The Grandmother and Her Bike
140 The Grandmother at the Surgery
140 The Grandmother and Her Grandson
141 The Grandmother in Her Frilly Dress
141 The Grandmother and the Pool Attendant
141 The Grandmother's Sofa
142 The Grandson's Teeth
142 The Grandmother and Sky-diving
142 The Grandmother and the Tweed Coat
143 The Grandmother and the Rat
143 The Grandmother and a Member of the Public
144 The Grandmother at the Station
144 The Grandmother and Her Visitors
145 The Grandmother in the Shower-room
145 The Grandmother's Birthday
145 The Grandmother in Bed
146 The Grandmother's Unbearable Mortification
146 The Grandmother in the Road
146 The Grandmother's Hair
147 The Grandmother at the Pharmacy
147 The Grandmother's Knees
147 The Grandmother Upstairs
148 The Grandmother in the Forest
148 The Grandmother and the Pears
148 The Grandmother on the Bus
149 The Grandmother's Neck
149 The Grandmother and the Wives of Violent Men
149 The Grandmother in a Sombrero
150 The Grandmother's Frock

150 The Grandmother and the Doctor's Thigh
150 The Grandmother's Shoes
151 The Grandmother's Smile
151 The Boredom of the Late Pool Attendant
151 The Grandmother and Her Enormous Children
152 The Grandmother and the Murderers
152 The Grandmother's New Home
152 The Grandmother's New Friends
153 The Grandmother and the Goose
153 The Grandmother in Her Room
153 The Grandmother and Her Apples
154 The Grandson and the Doctor
154 The Grandmother on the Lawn
154 Grandmother's Chins
155 The Grandmother and the Counsellors
155 The Grandmother Paints Her Face
155 The Grandmother Laughs
156 The Grandmother at the Grand Hotel
156 The Grandmother and her Greetings Cards
156 The Grandmother at Night
157 The Grandmother in the Flower Bed
157 The Grandmother Enjoys Her Tea
157 The Grandmother Goes for a Walk
158 The Grandmother's Bell
158 The Grandmother at Mealtimes
158 The Grandmother and the Sound of Laughter
159 The Grandmother and Erling Haaland
160 Flocks of Sheep
160 The Grandmother Who Loved to Chat

**MEN IN SHORTS**

163 Men
163 Springtime
163 The Woman with the Corgi
164 Husbands
164 The Nice Cow

164 The Neapolitan Mastiff
165 Several Lovers
165 The Priest
165 Brothers
166 The Tall Policeman
166 Nishikori
166 Manliness
167 The Letter
167 The Sea
167 The Tiny Reed Warbler
168 Drowning
168 Power-boats
168 Motherhood
169 The Genius
169 Wild Flowers
169 A View of the Sea
170 Playing Cricket in the Mist
170 Cathedral
170 What It's Like to Ride a Cow
171 The Flautist
171 Huskies
171 What My Mother Said
172 Jealousy
172 Dentistry
172 The Beard
173 Little Rabbits
173 BBQ
173 The Tubby Whippets
174 Rain
174 The Terrible Mess
174 Fathers
175 Running
175 Love
175 The Mysterious Man
176 Visitors
176 The Woman with the Lab

176 Cows
176 Our Plans for Today
177 The Man from Cheshire
177 The Word Mistress
177 The Musician
178 The Adorable Man
178 Summertime

**BONKERS**

181 The Afghan Hound
181 The Basset Griffon Vendeens
181 The Basset Hound
181 The Bichon Frise
181 The Boxer
181 The Bulldog
183 The Cavalier King Charles Spaniel
183 The Chow
183 The Chihuahua
184 The Cocker Spaniel
184 The Collie
184 Corgis
185 The Dachshunds
185 The English Bull Terrier
185 The German Shepherd
186 The German Short-haired Pointer
186 The German Wire-haired Pointer
186 The Gordon Setters
187 The Great Dane
187 The Hungarian Vizsla
187 The Irish Wolfhounds
188 The Jack Russell Terriers
188 The Kerry Blue
188 The Lurcher
189 The Mastiff
189 The Miniature Poodles
189 The Patterdale

190 The Pomeranian
190 The Rhodesian Ridgeback
190 The Saluki
191 The Scottish Terrier
191 The Setters
191 The Sheltie
192 The Shih Tzus
192 The Springer Spaniel
192 The Standard Poodle
193 The Stray
193 The Weimaraner
193 The West Highland Whites
194 The Whippet
194 The Yorkshire Terrier

**UNTIL THE TEARS ROLL DOWN MY CHEEKS LIKE HONEY**

196 The One-legged Man
196 Birdsong
197 His Dusty Jacket and His Ice-cold Hands
197 Being Looked at by a Man Standing Very Close Beside Me
198 The Tall Giraffe
198 The Mystery of My Submission
199 Menswear
199 Please Can He Not Know a Thing about Me
200 What Other People Think
200 Sitting on the Bench like a Snail
201 Jesus and the Radios
201 Two Strangers in a Field with Some Sheep
202 My Private Life
202 It Hasn't Stopped Raining For Days
203 Please Don't Answer *Chess*
203 Alone with Me
204 The Golden Lion
204 I Need a Haircut and I Need It Now
205 The Hide-out in the Mountains
205 Between the Devil and the Deep Blue Sea

205 Never Mention Mother
206 Bobby Fischer's Eyes
206 The Sun Will Rise Tomorrow
206 It's Possible to Walk in the Countryside
207 A Visit to the Grave of the Dancer
207 A Snowy Afternoon in December
208 A Slice of Cake Wrapped in Silverfoil
208 Everything About Him
209 Angry Golfers, Sinister Children
209 St Catherine of Siena and her Ring
210 My Big Worry
210 *Everybody Loves Me*
210 So Woebegone, So Flabby, So Alone
211 The Smile, When It Comes...
211 A Jumble of Old Radios
211 My Controversial Theory about Bobby Fischer
212 The Aeroplane
212 The Disappearing Mouse
212 Fantasy Involving a Hairbrush
213 How to Share a Banana
214 A Boring Man
214 A Man and a Woman on a Bench
214 Please Don't Be Afraid to Meet My Eye
215 The Man Who Didn't Sleep
215 The Man is Gone
216 Dachshunds
217 The Day He Took His Jacket Off
217 Outside the Golf Club Car Park on a Windy Day
218 Kafka's Fear of Mice

**THE SURLY MOTHERS OF SUCCESSFUL MEN**

220 The Bungalow (1)
220 Palazzo Trousers
220 Ants (1)
220 My Uncle's Private Parts
221 My Mother-in-Law Comes to Tea

221 The Boulder
221 Culottes
221 The Leg of the One-legged Jockey
221 Father (1)
222 The Man in Pyjamas
222 Wedding Day
222 Fountains
222 Foible
222 The Woman in the Purple Trousers
223 Walking Backwards
223 The Visitor Regards My Big Black Dog
223 The Surly Mothers of Successful Men (1)
223 The Dirty Look
223 The Electricity Sub-station
224 What to Teach Your Children
224 The Little Stone
224 The Man with Undyed Hair
224 The Other Person
224 Ears
225 The Wounds of Successful Men
225 Heatwave
225 The Leftover Sausages
225 Buckinghamshire
225 Roger Federer in Switzerland
226 Question (1)
226 The Visit to the Care Home
226 Uncles
226 The Doctor's Question I Found So Hard to Answer
226 Women with Straight Hair
227 Bathmat
227 Bodies in the Snow
227 The Things He Says
227 The Holiday
228 The Residents
228 Gentleness
228 The Letter H

228 Salt
229 My Uncle's Cooking
229 The Sister Who Didn't Exist
229 Mouth
230 The Bungalow (2)
230 The Doctor's Hands
230 Lip Balm
230 Girls Who Disobey
231 Pineapple Shampoo
231 The One-legged Jockey and the Cook
231 Cacti
231 My Mother's Bed
232 The Knife
232 Timetables
232 Well-meaning Actions
232 Advice to the Reader
232 My Earliest Memory
233 Chicken
233 Symptoms
233 All My Endless Questions
233 The Orange Dress
233 The Aunt and Her Dog
234 Question (2)
234 The Lost and Found Dog Disc
234 At the Pool (1)
234 The Visitor
234 Screams (1)
235 The Sort of Person Who
235 The Man Who Was Crying
235 The Letter B
235 A Love of Punctuation
235 But What's It Like?
236 Person Talking While Standing in the Sea
236 Her Small Son
236 Woman in a Wetsuit
236 Snakes

237 Bereavement (1)
237 Tuesdays
237 Density
237 The Library at Night
237 Screams (2)
238 The Girl Made of Glass
238 Bausch
238 The Telephone Call
238 Hope
239 The Man Who Taught Me Greek
239 The Man Shouting into His Phone
239 Question (3)
239 Women Carrying Bowls
239 Bluebell
240 My Inability to Drive
240 The Same for Everyone
240 Somewhere in Lincolnshire
240 Prayer (1)
240 Her Mother's Cheek
241 The Poodle
241 The Timetable
241 The Interesting Tumble-dryer
241 The Elephant Kanchenjunga
241 Prayer (2)
242 The Stolen Tennis-ball
242 There's Nothing Wrong with Ducks
242 The Widower at Night
242 In the Garden Shed when the Door Slams Shut
242 The Date
243 The Bungalow (3)
243 Child in a Flat
243 Humiliation
243 The Little Play
243 Granny and the Cloud
244 La Belle Hélène
244 Little Things Are Happening All the Time

244 Man in the Street
244 The Outing
244 Question (4)
245 The Dream of the Dreamer
245 My Dog at 9 a.m.
245 The Sound of Breaking Glass
245 The Surly Mothers of Successful Men (2)
246 The Shimmering Lake
246 Mum and the Fly
246 Ironmonger
246 September Evenings at My Grandmother's
246 Me-Time
247 Mary (1)
247 His Other Girlfriend
247 The New Cardigan
247 The Most Interesting Thing About Me
248 Heaven
248 The Prefab
248 Mrs P.
249 Strawberry Jam
249 Who I Am
249 The Stranger's Car
249 Smoothie at Midnight
249 Bereavement (2)
250 To the Reader
250 Fun
250 Question (5)
250 As I Tried to Explain Years Later
250 What I Asked the Person Standing Next to Me
251 China Blue
251 The Hearty Breakfast
251 The Blessed Virgin Mary Goes Swimming
251 He Told Me To Make a List (1)
251 The Surly Mothers of Successful Men (3)
252 Ants (2)
252 Weight

252 The Kitten
252 Spiders
252 My Sister's Hair
252 Cucumber
253 He Told Me To Make a List (2)
253 Prayer (3)
253 The Problems of Taking It in Turns
253 At the Pool (2)
253 The Irish Terrier and the Irish Terrier's Owner
254 Thicket
254 On Passing a Field with 7 Cows and 7 Sheep in It
254 The Bungalow (4)
254 Yes
254 Two Cows in a Meadow
255 You and Me
255 The Clinical Psychologist (1)
255 My Friends
255 The Surprise Birthday Present
255 My Grandmother's Dressing-gown
256 Zvuv
256 The Clinical Psychologist (2)
256 B. on Honeymoon
256 A & E
256 Things She Wishes She Had Brought on Holiday
257 Clairvoyance
257 My Dentist's Eyes
257 The Search
257 The General's Pyjamas
257 My Sister Whines
258 Purity of Heart
258 Wasps (1)
258 The Barista
258 The Woman with Thick Ankles
258 The Level Crossing
259 As the Bus Sails Past My Stop
259 My First Giraffe

259 Father (2)
259 My Own Mother
260 A Simple Question
260 The Woman in the Drawing-room
260 Mary (2)
260 What to Say
261 Apricot Lover
261 My Mother in Particular
261 Herons
261 Wasps (2)
261 The Clinical Psychologist (3)
262 Pins
262 The Child Within
262 The Man Who Walks 30 Miles a Day
262 Lambs
262 Cow at Night
263 The Birthday Present
263 Ice Hockey
263 Question (7)
263 The Bishop Digs a Hole
263 Sideboard
264 The Bungalow (5)
264 The Peacock
264 Birds
264 The Loving Hand
265 Happy Birthday
265 The Parrot
265 Golf
265 Omelette
266 The Right Amount of Smiling
266 The Man Who Doesn't Want To Be Forgiven
266 The Happy Couple
266 My Sister Accuses Me of Being an Attention-seeker
266 Faith
267 Mayonnaise
267 The Spoon (Testing My Powers of Observation)

267 The Cold Fish
268 Cookie
268 The Burning House
268 The Bungalow (6)

271 NOTES & ACKNOWLEDGEMENTS

# SELF-PORTRAIT WITH A BUCKET

## Self-portrait with an Armadillo

The armadillo hasn't got a clue
who I am, and nor does he care:

it's hard enough to care about himself
and how to roll himself into a ball.

## Self-portrait with a Bathmat

I'm in a misty valley with no clothes on,
alone but for a white, rectangular sheep.

## Self-portrait with a Beautiful Face

In this next portrait we see me –
or, rather, what we see is my body

but with a superimposed
beautiful face.

## Self-portrait with the Blessed Virgin Mary

Mother? Really? How does that work?
And why does your poor baby look so long?
And why is it you're always sitting down
and never standing up or doing anything?
How come you never even change your clothes?
What's the problem? Why be 'blessed'? Why take it?
And what's the point of being blessed anyway?

## Self-portrait with a Book

My cousin
(who is very shy)
is asking me

to please ignore
his hard-on
so I'm reading.

## Self-portrait with My Brother

Not so much a man as a giraffe –
if you can imagine a giraffe

sitting in an armchair
studying Yiddish.

## Self-portrait with a Bunch of Roses in Front of My Face

I'm holding them in front of my face
not, as you might think, to sniff them better

nor to look more closely at the petals
but because I have succumbed to shame.

## Self-portrait as a Corpse

When I am a corpse I will regret
my four tattoos – as she said I would.

Cold and shrunk.
Not a good look.

## Self-portrait with a Cowpat

Beyond the garden lies a green field
and in the field live enormous cows

and one fine day I take my sister's doll
and sink it with a stick into a cowpat.

## Self-portrait with Crawling Mothers

There's no such thing as well-intentioned wasps,
there's no such thing as ostriches that sing,

there's no such thing as being unaffected by
the sight of mothers crawling on their knees.

## Self-portrait with a Crown of Thorns

The crown of thorns is not on my head.
I'm holding it in my hands and walking
down the path to the compost heap
where the snake is sunning itself.

## Self-portrait in a Cupboard

I'm sitting in a cupboard with my dog.
You can see my arms round his neck.

He likes it here with me in this cupboard.
What he does not like is the paraglider.

## Self-portrait with Curly Hair, Holding a Mushroom

I was so afraid of being poisoned
that if I touched a mushroom I would pray –

something that was strictly forbidden
by my father when I was a child.

Not only would he watch me, he would touch me.
I think he was distracted by my hair.

## Self-portrait as Their Daughter

When I was their daughter
they made clear

I wasn't worth the trouble
when first one

and then the other, shattered,
passed away.

## Self-portrait, Deep in Thought

It seems to be some kind of tournament.
Rows and rows of boards have been set up

and hundreds of happy little pieces
are busy playing chess. All by themselves!

The hall has got no windows. That's because
the hall is not a hall, it's my head.

## Self-portrait with a Doe

'Self-portrait with a Doe'? But why the doe?
To see if I can learn to be more lovable

or anyway to see if I can learn
to be like how a doe would not be frightened by.

## Self-portrait as a Duck

They called me
'Nude'.
I'd rather be a duck.

## Self-portrait as a Footballer, Carrying a Bucket

Curly-haired women can't kick;
curly-haired women get tickled;

curly-haired women sometimes plunge
their curly heads into ice-cold water.

## Self-portrait with a Furious Headmaster

The furious headmaster,
the priest,
the Bouvier de Flandres,
the man upstairs –
which one even is my father
anyway?

## Self-portrait in Goggles

When I get too bored of being vertical
I strap my goggles on and count to five;

I slice the icy water like a knife
(albeit in goggles) slicing liver.

## Self-portrait with a Hammer

Yes, I am aware that people wonder
why I walk about with this hammer

but what I think these people underestimate
is how much joy whacking people brings.

## Self-portrait with a Hornet

My sister was terrified of hornets.
I made a sign: HORNETS WELCOME HERE!

## Self-portrait with My Husband

My husband is eating a banana.
How can someone eating a banana
look so grumpy?

But I say nothing.
Nor do I mention – why would I? –
the spiders that lurk in the bananas.

## Self-portrait with a Jelly on My Head

It's hard to be polite when all the time
I'm balancing a jelly on my head

that falls apart, I think it's calves-foot jelly;
sometimes the whole calf is on my head,

plaintively
mooing in my ear.

## Self-portrait in a Jumbo Jet

I'm either not alone in the cockpit
or it isn't true I can't fly.

## Self-portrait in the Kitchen with a Spoon

Taramasalata, golden syrup,
drowning beetles, Calpol, double cream.

## Self-portrait with a Lettuce

His visits make me sick!
I'm like a fugitive
after a huge plane has flown over:

the fugitive
was planting lettuces.
The grey-green plane was flying much too low.

## Self-portrait at the Lido

I'm lying in the rain feeling sick.
The throbbing of the pump does my head in.

Is it true Nijinsky was autistic?
Nothing really matters except hygiene.

## Self-portrait with a Mosquito

It reappears
and stabs me in the cheek

although I have done nothing.
Just lain here.

## Self-portrait with My Mother-in-Law

My mother-in-law places a coaster
on the little shelf above my chair

but then I put my cup – I'm so nervous! –
beside the coaster, where there's no room.

## Self-portrait as Myself

If it seems incredibly self-regarding
that's because it is.
But it's fun!

When I used to sit for other people
it wasn't fun at all.
It was wrong.

## Self-portrait with My Neighbour Who Doesn't Like Swimming

My neighbour is fed up with his swimming pool.
He says he doesn't even like swimming!

If it was mine, I'd drain out all the water
and fill the pool with raw and shell-less oysters

to see what it would feel like to swim
not through water but through raw oysters.

## Self-portrait in 1975

None of the 'exhaustive'
obituaries
of our late father
mention us.
By 'us' I mean
his sub-standard daughters.

## Self-portrait with Novak Djokovic

Here I am with Novak Djokovic.
(This portrait is obviously imaginary!)

He's nibbling at a hard-boiled egg
but what he really wants is my Black Forest gâteau.

## Self-portrait in a Pair of Expensive Italian High Heels

Only joking. That should be 'Self-portrait
Never in a Million Years Seen Wearing

the Kind of Shoes my Sister used to Wear'.
Much too high. In a good way.

## Self-portrait with a Pair of Tweezers

After I had killed it
I was sorry
and carved a giant tick
in its honour
and set it on a plinth
on a mountain-top
and everybody marvelled
at its beauty
(while secretly wishing
ticks were herbivores).

## Self-portrait with a Pan of Tomato Sauce

In the pan of warm tomato sauce
you can see a school of naked women

floating on their backs among the onions
because they have surrendered to derangement.

## Self-portrait with a Parrot on My Shoulder

Why is there a parrot on my shoulder
when, number one, I am not a pirate

and, number two,
I prefer lips.

## Self-portrait with Parsley

My mother was easily upset
and omelettes upset her most of all.

Everything had to be just right.
She even rejected the perfect ones.

## Self-portrait in a Peach-coloured Bath

I haven't slashed my wrists.
I'm not a duck.

I'm not Ophelia.
I am a resident

residing
in a seaside hotel.

## Self-portrait as a Pebble

I'm not the only pebble on the beach
but I'm the only one I know first-hand.

And it's the same for all the other pebbles:
we know ourselves; we cannot know each other.

## Self-portrait with a Piglet

I'm wriggling on my sofa with a piglet –
a cross between a piglet and a two-year-old –

listening to the drumming of the rain
and trying both to tickle and count backwards.

## Self-portrait as a Pilot

I 'divide my time' between writing
and flying light aircraft for lepidopterists.

(The name 'Selima Hill' is a pseudonym:
I prefer anonymity.)

## Self-portrait with a Pound of Flesh

I've cut this pound of flesh from my thigh
and dressed the wound with the stiffened frills

(the stiffened frills now blood-stained) of the tutu
that little girls like me were forced to flutter in.

## Self-portrait in a Restaurant

The woman in the skin-tight dress is saying
she likes to feel penetrated!

Silence.
Then the other woman starts to cry.

## Self-portrait in a Sauna

Please can someone sit me in a sauna
and leave me there, alone with the heat,

like a huge potato on its wedding-day
that sits beside its huge potato loved one,

very close,
with nothing to do.

## Self-portrait at the Seaside

This bucket is for sand
and not for octopi

and nor is it appropriate for someone
looking for a place to take her clothes off in.

## Self-portrait in Several Harnesses

I'm dressed in several tight leather harnesses.
a cardboard skirt down to my ankles,

ankle-weights, wrist-weights and a hood
because I have been dressed by my mother.

## Self-portrait with a Shoe

When he comes and knocks against my shoe
I think the tortoise loves me but he doesn't.

## Self-portrait in the Shower

Many people wouldn't understand
but I'm afraid of showers
because showers
hurt my nipples
like a shower of pins,
of villainous and acrobatic pins.

## Self-portrait in a Side Room

Soon I will be lying on my back –
undressed, afraid, with my legs apart –

saying to myself this too will pass
as if to say this too will pass will help.

## Self-portrait as a Sock

When I was unborn I was as baffling
as badly loaded lorry-loads of newts,

as blameless and as crumpled as a sock;
as stern, as unexpected, as reality.

## Self-portrait Standing in a Queue Beside a Businessman

I wonder if this person is a businessman.
And what do businessmen even do?

He looks at me as if he knows I'm thinking
he's not a man I'd pour my heart out to!

And what do I myself do all day long?
As if it all makes sense when it so doesn't.

## Self-portrait with Straightened Hair

And this is me straightening my hair!
I wonder what God thinks. And if He prays.

And, if He does, does He pray for me?
And will He pray for my long-suffering hair?

And what is 'pray' supposed to mean, anyhow?
To me, to pray is not to pray but whinge.

## Self-portrait with a Tin of Golden Syrup

Because they have refused to accept
certain things about myself they hate,

when I am alone I can't resist
pouring golden syrup into my bunches.

## Self-portrait with the Toenail of a Saint

Because I'm kneeling meekly in my uniform,
pressed against the statue of the Virgin

by all the other little girls in uniform,
no one knows how murderous I am.

## Self-portrait as a Tufty-eared Red River Hog

An expert at wallowing and rooting,
my aim is to submerge myself in mud

so nobody can gawp at me or smell me
or think they can identify my grunts.

## Self-portrait with an Umbrella

I'm holding the umbrella for a witch.
She's struggling up the steps
of a caravan
where I can see a jar of boiled sweets
that may or may not
be or have been
poisoned.

## Self-portrait, Undressed

When I was twelve years old I got undressed
and modelled for a so-called 'family friend' –

and here I am, in that same pose,
laden, like a tree with fruit, with rage.

## Self-portrait with an Unknown Man

Who this person is
I've no idea

but I do recognise
the shoes –

if shoes like that
can be called shoes.

## Self-portrait with a Wall

I'm knocking at a door in a wall,
a six-foot wall that used to be my mum.

I can knock as hard as I like,
the six-foot wall refuses to respond.

## Self-portrait with X in the Dark Woods

Because you looked as if you thought I'd hurt you,
much to my surprise I stroked your hand.

# THE MATHEMATICIAN

## Classic Cars

Like Charlie Watts, the drummer,
who can't drive
but nevertheless collects classic cars,
I know what I want to say
but I never say it.

## The Cake

I don't know if you've ever iced a cake
but if you have you'll know how long it takes.
A steady hand, and a wet knife.
The cake itself's completely ignored by me,
or anyway I do the best I can
at completely ignoring the man
so as not to frighten him.

## Bear

A stone-cold bear with a heart of stone
that, if it wasn't cold, would be violent.

## Having to Remember Every Day

Having to remember every day
he's still the person
he forgets he was,
who anyway
he doesn't want to think about,
and doesn't want to be,
or have once been,
unfortunately makes him bad-tempered.

## The Picnic

I know, I know, I'm getting on his nerves,
he doesn't listen to a word I'm saying,
I talk too much,
I ask too many questions,
jabber, jabber, jabber, on I go,
I fuss about, doing God knows what,
for ever wasting everybody's time,
can't decide which shoes to wear, and, yes,
I ask too many questions, all the time,
I haven't got a clue what to order,
or what it's like to have to be kept waiting;
my precious little plants are so much clutter,
the fruit I eat is dribbly and uneatable,
and, as the poor man knows to his cost,
there's nothing I like better than to swim –
without providing rugs or a proper picnic –
out to the horizon, while he waits,
abandoned to the never-ending dunes.

## Far into the Night

Far into the night
the angry man
hunches in the glow of his computer screen.

## Friends

Because his friend's depressed
and not much company
the mathematician
simply avoids him.

## Violins and Salad

I play the violin and violins
are probably his least favourite things.
Violins and salad. Too girly.
Hidden in the vaults of mathematics,
anything more girly is too much for him.

## The Mathematician and the Parrot

He says she lets it shit all over the house
and steal his food
and rip up all his curtains
and all because of the woman's misguided gratitude
to the man who owned the parrot
and what he did for her.

## Friendship

It's nothing to do with me he says crossly
and walks away to find another friend.

## The Value of Difficult People

The value of our so-called 'difficult people' –
of the friend in question, for example –
is, like the beach at night,
underestimated.

## What He Likes About His New Home

He likes the way nobody smiles
and nobody's expected to smile.
He also likes the fact you can't hear geese.

## Sunshine

All he wants to do is do nothing
but sit there in his car and drive around
and curse the other drivers, curse pedestrians,
the sunshine in his eyes,
the politicians,
and when I say 'curse' I mean glare,
he's much too civilised to actually curse,
he doesn't say a word, and half the time
he doesn't seem to know where he's going,
know or care,
or why he's going there,
or who we are
or what it is he's eating
that some kind person in the back seat
is handing round,
some thoughtful cook
(not me).

## Eels

Luckily,
sometimes I sit still,
but sometimes, on the contrary, like today,
I wriggle like a sack full of eels.

## The Meeting

The more he says he can't wait to see me
the more I am reluctant to be seen.

## Buns

At the time it seemed to me more friendly
to get one each
but now it seems less friendly
as I sit and watch him eat them both.

## The Man on the Sofa (1)

I disapprove of lots of things, he says.
In fact, he adds, I disapprove of you.

## Bananas

Explaining that he's bought himself some fresher ones,
he offers me a bunch of brown bananas.

## Dogs and Bears

One of my favourite occupations
is throwing them unwanted teddy bears
then watching them tearing them to pieces –
an occupation he remains unmoved by.

## The Angry Man

Why is he so grumpy all the time?
I am not 'grumpy', he replies,
I'm angry.

## Girls Like Me

He doesn't like the skin on his forearms,
people who don't pass their test first time,
mugs with too small bases,
girls like me
and dogs named after Conservative politicians.

## Doing Something Drastic About My Hair

Luckily he doesn't seem to notice
my idiotic curls (it's the weather),
he doesn't even notice how the neighbours
park their Saab where Mother's planted cyclamen
(cyclamen! her favourite!) and luckily
he shambles past it like a sort of bear,
a cross between a bear and a toad,
with hands like paws,
flat-footed, inarticulate,
that's not, and never can be said to be,
a cuddly bear, in spite of all the wool –
the unwashed blankets piled in the back,
the woolly hat,
its stupid woolly bobble –
no, he's more like one of those black bears
that roam through built-up neighbourhoods at night
stealing snacks,
stealing more than snacks,
which doesn't mean to say they should be 'culled'
('culled' means killed by the way): like us,
like you and me, they will respond to love...
And now I can't put off any longer
doing something drastic about my hair.

## The Emperor

When we're going somewhere,
just the two of us,
we never walk along side by side
like couples are supposed to do, no,
he has to walk miles up in front
as if he is an emperor or something.

## Vermiculite (1)

I wish some patient person
would explain
what vermiculite is
without groaning.

## And Another Question

He always says I ask
'too many questions' –
but how many questions
are 'too many' questions?

## The Man on the Sofa (2)

What is he annoyed about?
Everything!
And, saying that,
he rolls onto the floor.

## The Fence

A woman with a ribbon in her hair
or, even worse, a flower in her hair,
is 'beyond the pale', he declares.
(A pale is a kind of wooden fence.)

## The Colour of the Cushion

Why do we dislike certain colours?
The cushion he's appeared with, for example:
I'm trying to make the fact that it's from him
override the fact I hate the colours.

## The Upside-down Dog

Why's the little dog upside down?
Does he want his fur to smell of stone?
Or does he want the stone to smell of fur?
Is his shoulder itchy? Is he praying?
Is it something sexual or something?
He says Don't worry but I'm not worried!
On the contrary, I like it here:
I'm interested in upside-down dogs.

## The Graceless Man

When I suggest he makes his tea himself
the graceless man replies he can't be bothered.

## The Yellow Lorry

Worried?
I'm not worried!
I'm excited
to find myself behind a yellow lorry
with HUB LE BAS painted on the side.

## The Driver

Idiot! he mutters,
you've just wasted
sixteen seconds
of my precious life!

## The Anniversary

The man I'm trying to please
grabs the menu,
puts it down ungraciously
and groans.

## The Visitors

I even brought them back to the house
and that was when it happened,
not surprisingly.

## The Nursery

Inside the nameless friend
there is a nursery
where babies with no mothers
fail to thrive.

## The Meaning of Barf

Well, I say, what does it sound like?
He neither knows nor cares what it sounds like.

## The Clap of Thunder

Why would you call an inn 'The Clap of Thunder'?
Don't ask me!
We've sat here long enough.

## Persian Primer

I and the Emperor conversed in the garden.
His son bore envy while his sisters wept.
In the garden sang a nightingale.
I'm sorry my 'plus-one' is so bad-tempered.

## Helping Others

There are those
it feels good to help;
others, not so much,
unfortunately.

## My Friend in the Woolly Hat

He wears a woolly hat
and in winter
he even wears the woolly hat in bed;
he lives on tinned potatoes and tinned peaches
and says he's far too busy to be kind.

## The Nose

The man I try to please
or, if not please,
the man I try, at least, to understand
is lying in the sun
with his nose burnt.

## The Bear Woman

Stuffed so tight she can't even move.
So far from home she can't, or won't, remember
where that might have been.
Beyond numb.

## Dogs and Mathematicians

If dogs could talk
they'd talk about smells;
mathematicians
talk about maths.

## Vermiculite (2)

Of course I know it's not vermicelli
and baby worms are not baby worms.

## Bras in the Sun

First I peg my bras up on the line
and then, in case he comes,
I take them down again,
and, when he fails to come,
I peg them up again.

## The Whistling Man

The whistling man's so cheerful!
We both are!
When we meet
he goes *You've made my day!*

## Sunday Afternoon

The fact is he must sense
he's being treated
as someone kind of shabby
I don't trust.

## Violence

Violence tiptoes in and out of rooms
and in and out of people's legs
like rats,
rats that store the kind of violent sorrow
that blights the lives of disappointed men

## Sleep

The friend alone
is like a beach at night
when rocks dissolve
and fish lie down to sleep.

## What I'm Trying to Say

What I'm trying to say is
he's so kind
when I, I know, am rarely kind to him.
Sometimes kind;
sometimes more like brutal.

# A MAN, A WOMAN & A CHIHUAHUA

## A Man, A Woman and a Crossword Puzzle

She couldn't sleep until she'd got the answer. *Actually,* he *said, I don't care.* The answer was ESCHEW. It often is.

## A Man, A Woman and a Piece of Cake

Anyway, I'm not going to tell you after all, the woman says. Why not, says the man. You're in a bad mood, says the woman. I'm always in a bad mood, says the man and prods her cake.

## A New Pair of Boots

I said how much I liked her new boots. I didn't like them one little bit. And they looked as if they didn't like *me*.

## Annabel

Finally they reached a decision: they agreed to call their child Moose. Or, if she was a girl, to call her Mousse. It was a girl. They called her Annabel.

## Bring Nadine

Yes, she cried, *you're welcome, bring Nadine, bring the lot*, but they didn't come.

## But People Do Love You

But people do love you, says the doctor. Many people.

*Many people?* Well, it's not enough. And if you don't believe me you're an idiot.

## Can I Get You Something?

Can I get you something? Tea? Coffee? Do sit down. Make yourself at home. No, not there. Can I wash your face? Does it feel good? Please leave.

## Cooked Breakfasts and Shrieks

I came here to get away from cooked breakfasts. Cooked breakfasts make me feel sick. Let others cook them and eat them but, please, not here. And another thing, which, again, may suit some people but not others: the shrieks as naked heiresses hit the water.

## Dead Flies

Does a spider ever get bored? Do they drink? Can they see the sun? Do the flies they catch beg for mercy? Or do the flies feel honoured to be eaten? Do you ever feel like eating *me*?

That'll do, Suzette, says the doctor.

You call yourself a doctor! yells Suzette, and hurls the trembling doctor over the cliff she's pleased to see conveniently nearby.

## Dinner with My Father

My father is sitting at the table eating meat. He looks at me as if I am a chair.

After dinner he looks at me again. He's like a surgeon with no glasses on.

## Eggs

One of the smaller towels has gone missing. I say this can't go on but it can. I'll leave him hard-boiled eggs underneath the bucket.

## Expensive Cheeses

His daughter always brings him expensive cheeses – and he likes expensive cheeses – but he's going to need more than expensive cheeses with a foot like this!

## Field Guide to Spiders of Britain and Northern Europe

There are guides to Fish, to Coastal Wildlife, the Seashore, Shells, Knots, Seabirds, Insects, Mammals, Butterflies and Moths but none to Spiders. Next time I come I will bring a guide to Spiders. (The more choice I have, the more *anxious* I become, so I will bring only one, small guide.)

## Friendly People

You can't say things like that to friendly people, people who have no way of knowing what happened, so I say *Hi!*

## He's Got More Money Than He Knows What To Do With

Well, maybe he has, she says, but she's not interested.

## His Ebullient Aunt's Latest Adventures in Eastern Europe and the Third World

To his ebullient aunt's long message about her latest adventures in Eastern Europe and the Third World, he replied *Whatever.*

## His Little Sausage

But what if the special teacher stops coming? What if the boy stops eating altogether? She says the teacher calls him *His Little Sausage.*

## Home

I didn't ask too many questions and we agreed he wouldn't make a mess, he wouldn't snore, and he wouldn't eat me. He seemed to be a friendly sort of lion.

## Ice Cream and Jelly

The light is on in my neighbour's bedroom. I used to see him feeling his way with a stick. He, too, can't sleep… When I was a child, my piano teacher called my jelly *eye-balls*.

## Impatience

I wish my visitor would hurry up and visit because I am cold in this little cardigan and I want to wear the one that comes down to my ankles.

## It Hasn't Stopped Raining for Days

It hasn't stopped raining for days and, as a precaution, we've put the parrot and his perch upstairs. The garden and the drive are under water.

## J.

She wrote her name on a piece of paper. I said it was a very nice name.

Most women I know will talk about their father willingly, but not J.

## Mary

Mary is lying on the floor with her eyes shut. She is trying to summon up the energy to reach her pillow but so far without success.

## Midnight

After he had gone I sat on the sofa and ate ice cream. I DO NOT LIKE being shouted at. I prefer men being gentle with me.

## My Bony Hands

Bony, mauve, subservient, my hands could be the hands my mother wrung for me.

## My Miserable Sister

Is my sister more miserable when she says she is 'miserable' or when she says she is 'mizzy', like this morning?

## 'My Miserable Sister'

I'm thinking of writing a book which won't be a book exactly but a collection of the opening sentences of other books.

## Nudity

When I answered *Nudity*, the man, who said he was a doctor, didn't smile.

## Panthers

Women in short shorts and high-heeled sneakers, like women who bake cakes, who groom Chihuahuas, women who seem not to have a problem with electric blankets, Holy Water, bedding plants, women who reject supportive men, are not my type, but they are more my type than those who use live puppies to capture panthers.

## Peaburgers

Yes to peaburgers, yes to expandable clothing and cute baby elephants; labyrinths, bamboo clothes pegs, hubcaps and atolls; to large and small and medium-sized acrobats; mute and nameless surgeons; F2F. No to flint, to steeply shelving beaches, to dogs named after politicians; beeps, and names you can't pronounce and can't remember.

## PRIVATE

I'm sitting on some wooden steps marked PRIVATE when someone shouts *Can I squeeze past?* but then he sees what I'm doing. So, *no*.

## Roly

Two women are in a caravan. The first woman passes the second woman a photograph. In the photograph the second woman is sitting on a beach with a Golden Retriever on her lap. They both look fed up.

## Sardines

Not everyone likes yogurt. Some people – people who love cows – prefer toast. The doctor and his butler like sardines, especially chocolate sardines.

## Sex with Jockeys

He'd tell me all these stories about sex (including sex with jockeys!). So yes, I naturally assumed it was me. It never crossed my mind it could be her.

## Sheep

I am writing this letter to explain about the sheep. I could sit here happily all day if it wasn't for the sheep!

## Sin

No to sin, to Suckies, sleepy horses; yes to being someone he can trust.

## Swimming with the Banker

Everything was breaking. A shed looked as though it couldn't even be bothered to fall over. There were newts in the paddling pool and a broken notice, NO UNACCOMPANIED ADULTS, was lying in the grass. He hated every minute.

## The Afternoon of Her Arrival

It's not the case that I am easygoing.

## The Air in the Mountains

The air in the mountains makes all the difference! She wakes up every morning thinking *Yes*, I can do this. And she *can* do it.

## The Answer Is Yes

I ask myself if she could see us now, would she wish I wasn't here beside him? The answer is, unfortunately, yes.

## The Box of Chocolates

Nice to talk to you, the old man said. Then he told me to give him a box of chocolates.

## The Chocolate Chip Cookie That My Daughter Had Given Me

At the very moment that I sank my teeth into the chocolate chip cookie that my daughter had given me, it began to rain. Big drops rolled down the window-pane and onto the roses. I don't like roses. They remind me of my mother.

## The Ear

He came hurtling across the field straight across to me and I picked him up and carried him home on my shoulders and it was only later I was told about the ear and how the children found it.

## The Empty Room

Things being dropped, doors being opened and closed. What sounds like the beating of wings. Then all is quiet.

The following morning he doesn't appear downstairs and there is no sign of him in his room.

## The Ewe

Tea from the communal urn is all very well but tea that is freshly made is certainly hotter! If it wasn't for tea and the ewe, he would be dead.

## The Famous Museum

My father went there nearly every day and that's why I wouldn't dream of ever going there – imagine bumping into him! No way! I know he's dead and everything but still.

## The Fox

I met a man who used to be a trucker and when he retired he bought himself a bungalow that had a fox living in the kitchen. *They lived on fox in Kazakhstan*, he said. *And elephant ears in a kind of stew*. And as he talked he dismembered wasps he trapped inside a jar smeared with honey.

## The Funeral

The funeral director asked me if the purple Porsche blocking the gateway belonged to me. Why would I need a purple Porsche? Why would I even want a purple Porsche? Who would pay for it, polish it, how? Why? After the funeral I saw a young blonde woman drive off in it. I know I shouldn't hate her.

## The Gift

Thank you for the gift and I hope you are well. I am writing to say it is best if you stop sending them. I know you will understand. Take care.

## The Hare

When he first got ill he blamed the flies – and it's true there were flies everywhere, big buzzy ones, but no one else got ill. I blame the hare.

## The Heart-throb

Little did I know when I married him that he had got three wives and a giraffe. He died and I adopted the giraffe.

## The Holiday-makers

This morning she positioned their garden chairs so that they could admire the horses and the sheep but this afternoon she has decided to move them somewhere else where they can't see them.

## The Key

I find the fact he didn't really weird. I myself would have picked it up and passed it to the lifeguard straightaway, radiant with compassion and efficiency.

## The Little Dog

A door opens and a man in large floral pyjamas appears and a little dog jumps out of a bush and runs inside.

## The Lonely Son

When his mother died he didn't speak. He didn't speak for nearly three days. Then he said in a loud voice *One o'clock and time for my dinner!*

## The Long Boring Journey

As a passenger I like to cheer him up but, when I say I wonder how many outdoor swimming pools there are in Paris, he doesn't answer.

## The Loony-bin

When my neighbour said he left his Volvo near 'the loony-bin', I didn't mention the night you climbed into the little park and 'took your life'. I mean, why would I?

## The Man in the Ugly Shoes

Little did she know that the man she avoided would be the man, many years later, she thinks she is falling in love with, in spite of the shoes.

## The Man Next Door

The man next door – he must have died years ago – used to sit on the step with a tea-towel over his head. When people asked her if he was okay, his wife (or maybe his daughter) said *Sure!*

## The Man with Four Dogs

Apparently the dogs aren't even his. They belong to the woman next door, who neglects them. This is how she now sees pain. Like *can it be avoided?* Answer: No.

## The Mental Health of Footballers

When the dancer smiled it made my day but we continued to talk about the mental health of footballers as if nothing had happened.

## The Orange Towel

The orange towel the man calls the brown towel, the words *generic*, *bulwark* and *egregious*, the fact that when someone says 'next Saturday' I never know if they mean this Saturday coming or the one after that, and if they mean this coming Saturday I wish they wouldn't keep calling it 'next Saturday' – they're all annoying, yes, but not as annoying as the fact that my sister still hasn't answered my letter. Oops – she's dead. Sorry, 'passed away'.

## The Perfect Coat

I tried wearing it as much as possible, hoping the sadness would wear off, but it didn't. Next time I go to a funeral I will wear something that I don't like that I won't want to wear again.

## The Picture of His Mother

The picture of his mother with a hippopotamus; złoty; personal hygiene – in that order.

## The Resident

Last night he came in at tea-time and went straight to bed. And now, this morning, I haven't the heart to go and wake him up. *Maybe he is ill.* But what do I know?

## The Sculpture

The man and woman look at the sculpture. The man doesn't like it. He says it is too physical. You mean too *erotic,* says the woman.

## The Singer

It turns out he didn't want to sing in the first place, and he is delighted to have a whole day to himself. And he walks towards the car with a shudder, a sort of gentle shudder she feels excluded by.

## The Sobbing Woman Lying on the Floor

While I am grasping her ankles she starts to sob. It seems to be doing her good. She sobs and sobs.

And now I want my own ankles grasped, very tightly, as I grasped hers.

## The Spider

*Don't worry about it,* he says irritably. But I'm not worried about it. On the contrary, I enjoy being stared at from behind the mugs.

## The Swimmer and the Man in a Tweed Coat

A woman in a red bikini walks out of the sea and onto a flat rock where she is met by a man in a tweed coat who passes her the cup of coffee he has been carrying along the beach towards her for the past fifteen minutes.

## The Visitor

One day a visitor knocked at the door. We offered her a biscuit which she ate. Then she told us why she had come. And then she took him away and it was over.

## The Woman by the River

Everything she touches is cold. She holds a fish as big as the baby. Even the baby is cold.

## The Woman Who Doesn't Smile

The woman who doesn't smile doesn't want to.

## Two Things I Know about the Hummingbird Hawk-moth

Everybody loves it. And two, it hovers with an audible hum. (I don't know if it only flies by day. Or if we can know good without evil.)

## Two Women I Don't Recognise

Two women I don't recognise walk into the changing-rooms, change into their swimming things and then, to my surprise, sit down. After maybe half an hour, they walk out again. I see them later in the car park and one of them is saying to the other *Listen, I don't want any flowers!*

## Two Women in a Restaurant

I don't know about you but what really annoys me about him is the way he starts eating his food before he's even sat down.

The other woman says *Don't look then.*

## Uncles

Uncles like to wear shoes that fit; they can, and do, think before breakfast; they specialise in mattresses and sauces; they book hotels, they fondle bridge rolls.

## Vodka

Saying I like vodka is like saying that 'brioches' is the name of a hairstyle.

## Wednesday Afternoon at the Lido

While the woman hammers up and down, her 'other half', with ducklings on his trunks, is busy spreading tenderness around us.

## Welcome Home

One of them, in a natty suit, and nearly six foot tall, is in the porch waiting to entangle me in silk.

## What Makes Me Happy

What makes me happy? My stepsister's nose. The fact that it is bigger than mine.

# BABY PETER

## The Tent

Overnight a tent has appeared.
Somebody is out there in the cold.

Whoever is inside it isn't moving.
If there *is* a person inside it.

Maybe they are scared, or asleep.
Or maybe they are too cold to move.

The pond beside the wood is frozen over.
In a perfect world it would be custard.

## Pig

Whoever put it there seems like a person
who needs to be a short sort of person,

either a person or a pig
who wakes up in the morning thinking *rosary*.

## Woman Alone in a Flat

He's never seen the countryside before,
all these trees, and he's so unfit,

and even walking here from the village,
he's sweating, and his feet are killing him,

but no, he says, he's never going back,
he didn't like the fighting, these people,

they kept on coming round to the flat
and telling him he had to go to college,

they kept on coming round, so he left,
he walked away, although he's not fit.

## Strawberry Jam

It hasn't stopped raining for days and not a soul
has passed the tent in which a large man
is cramming his face with chocolates from a bag...
Once a dog bit his mother's breast.
They dragged her off, kicking and screaming,

and he was left alone in the flat
for what seemed days,
eating strawberry jam,
and when she reappeared she smelled of streets,
she smelled of streets fourteen floors below

where tiny men and women in dark coats
who neither eat nor sleep
and have no names
and never know he's watching
come and go.

## The Waltzer

The way he talks, the way he hesitates,
he's like a waltzer learning how to waltz,
he talks as if he's not used to talking.

When he was eleven or twelve
his father died – and for the first time
he found himself living without fear.

He only drinks water or sweet tea.
Every day he walks into town
to wash his face and beard in hot water.

His auntie said his face was too big.
He says he left because of all the fighting.
He's like a waltzer waltzing in odd shoes.

## Cuckoo

Baby Peter was a big baby.
Much *too* big, to be honest.

Baby Peter's mother, on the contrary,
was small, like the host of a cuckoo,

like a bird –
but she couldn't fly.

## Baby Peter and the Cushions

His mother used to sit him on his mat
and try and prop him up with lots of cushions

but still she'd often find him fallen over,
waggling his short legs like a beetle.

## From His Bedroom on the Fourteenth Floor

From his bedroom on the fourteenth floor,
far beyond the houses and the reservoir –

so far away that if you spent your life
trying to reach it, you would never find it –

from his bedroom window, as a child,
he could see a land of green grass.

## A Good Boy

She was still at school when she had him.
On the floor. Just the two of them.

Did her mother help them? She did not.
Nobody, he says, enjoyed his company.

He was large and floppy like a beanbag.
His mother fed him cake soaked in milk.

She mashed the stale cake in a bowl
and stuffed his face till he fell asleep.

He never cried. Never made a fuss.
His mother used to say he was *a good boy*.

## The Verger's Toes

For seven days he lived in the churchyard.
When it rained he sheltered in the church.

He'd sit inside and watch with fascination
an elderly verger in black sandals.

## Baby Peter and the Rats

It's not that he is wilful. Far from it.
But he is big and heavy
like a sack.

It's like she's given birth to a sack,
a sack with two pink eyes, a dusty sack
that's full of something heavy like dead rats.

It's not that he's a monster
but he's big –
so big that he can't move, and she can't carry him.

## Miserable Owls

Where have they been hiding, those fat owls
hooting to each other in the woods?

Hooting about what? Are they happy?
Or, on the contrary, are they miserable?

Or don't they know? And anyhow who cares?
Voices. Dogs. All he wants is warmth.

## Baby Peter and the Good Shepherd

He spent his days in dressing-gown and slippers
like an old man. But he was four.

He kept his special bear in the pocket,
its orange fur stuck with boiled sweets.

He spent a lot of time in the corridor
chewing his big thumb till it was raw.

On Sundays she would dress him in a romper suit,
brush his hair, and wheel him into church

where someone gave him pictures of Mary,
or, if not Mary, of the Good Shepherd,

a man with long gold hair and a lamb.
(Either a man or a woman,
Baby Peter didn't really know.)

## Children in Go-karts

Sometimes children eat too much, he says,
and make a mess and when he was a boy

the other children used to harness him
and make him pull their go-karts till he bled.

He hasn't spoken to a child for years.
Children can be rather fat and noisy.

## The Reservoir

Every day he'd get his small bear,
small enough to fit inside his pocket,
and curl up on the floor and the teachers
would wake him up and send him straight home.
He had to get a job or go to college –
but you need to read to go to college.
After school he worked as a labourer.

Once he fell asleep, when it was snowing,
snowing hard, and when he woke up
somebody had taken the sandwich
his mother had put out the night before.
He was much bigger than his mother
and any time he could have picked her up
and thrown her like a stick into the reservoir.

## Baby Peter Lying on the Mat

Knitting. Cake. Toys on the floor.
Lying on the mat beside his bear.

Large and small women. Distant grass.
Somebody or something going *Hi!*

## Catalogues

His mother used to buy his clothes from catalogues.
He drank too much. He was bigger then.

People in the street would stare and shout.
*You never get used to it*, he says.

He only drinks tea now, or squash –
and squash he only drinks when it's raining.

## The Fight in the Snow

He talks about the fight in the snow,
that time, at work, he tried to get his sandwich back –

and maybe he was guilty, I don't know,
he said he wasn't but perhaps he was –

and then we are disturbed by, overhead,
the honking of innumerable geese.

## Orange Squash

Every night he checks the tent for spiders
but anyway at least they don't get drunk.

He himself only drinks tea.
Occasionally he'll have an orange squash

but then you get the wasps – and we agree
there's nothing we hate more than a wasp.

Once his mother pushed him to the pub
and poured a can of cider on his head

and soon he was standing on a wall
crawling with them like a wasp motel.

## The Accident

Yesterday he told me his father
didn't die of drink. Baby Peter
took his head and smashed it on the cooker.
He told the men it was an accident.
Now I don't know what to believe.

I thought his father died much earlier on.
Now he's saying he was seventeen.
Or maybe he is still alive somewhere,
an elderly law-abiding citizen
who only wants the best for his son.

## Beetle Mother

He slept all day – like one of those weird beetles
that navigate at night by the stars.

If she knew her son was in trouble –
if she knew or even thought she knew –

she also knew *It's none of my business.*
He wants to be rejected, she would say.

## To Be the Mother of a Helpless Baby

She'd no idea that it would be this hard
to be the mother of a helpless baby –

never mind
of a big man sobbing.

## Brothers for Peter

Alone at night lying in his tent
he wonders if he's got any brothers,

and if the brothers wonder about *him*.
He tries to stop himself but he fails.

## Pity

He stops. He starts. He stops again. He's sorry.
He's like a dancer dancing in tight shoes

as if he knows he ought to be enjoying it
but really he just wants to go home.

To pity him's not only not enough,
it isn't even kind, or appropriate.

## Pork

Maybe he is thinking of the owls
or maybe he is lying on his side

thinking nothing,
like a dead pig.

## Baby Peter's Orange Bear

Sometimes, in the night, when he's afraid,
he dreams about the small orange bear

and asks himself how come he let her go
and prays she's being cared for by someone.

## Baby Peter and the Doll

Baby Peter had a small bear.
He also had a big shiny doll.

It was dressed in thick woollen leggings
and given to him by the school cook.

Later on it wore a woollen dress
also knitted by the school cook.

She put a secret pocket inside
for him to keep its tiny missal in.

He loved to stroke the real pigskin cover
and, eyes half-closed, the silk of the ribbon.

## No One Ever Tells You

No one ever tells you it's this bad.
No one ever tells you, as a mother,

never to expect a child's gratitude.
No one ever tells you it's this lonely.

## Cake

He wants her to reject him
but she can't.

She can't for now
but she's working on it.

## Yellow Grass

I reached the woods at dawn
but all I found

was yellow grass
where the tent had been.

# AGATHA

## The Billionaire in his Office

The billionaire is sitting in his office.
No one else is allowed in.

*Absolutely not*. He checks his hairs,
the grey of which is never to be mentioned.

## Yachts at Sea

The only thing
the old are really good at –

they do it all the time,
in their thousands,

in houses, gardens, yachts at sea –
is age.

## In the Silence of the Hush

In the silence of the hush, a fly
investigates the lips of the sleeper;

it climbs onto her nose,
it looks around;

it taps her eyelid, like a tiny mouse
checking on the welfare of a loved one.

## Intimacy

Don't think about the thought of being intimate
and certainly don't think about the bodies,
don't think about the way they bruise like fruit;

what kind of fruit,
don't think about the fruit,
don't think about the fruit or the bruises,

don't think about the fingers
or the tips
that chill the fruit like carefully falling snowflakes.

## How Old is Old?

How old is old? As old as the hills?
All I know is, first, it's really nice

that all of us are growing old together
and, second, the importance of hygiene.

## Whippets

He didn't even want a dog anyway
but she insisted they would cheer him up

and now they've got these shivering little whippets
he's never going to find himself endeared by

any more than by unfolded veils,
their marble-like white bellies like white frogs'.

## Sunday Nights at the Care Home

They sleep by day
and roam about at night,

stealing from each other
as they go.

## Sadness

When the young are sad they get over it;
when the old are sad they never do.

## Soup

Alone in her vast kitchen
she makes soup

but when she sets it down in the dining-room
the billionairess is too bored to eat it.

## Old People in Tea-rooms

They squeeze themselves around the tiny tables,
arrange and rearrange their shiny bags

and never say the tables feel sticky
and never scrape their tiny sticky chairs.

## The Happy Faces of the Very Old

The happy faces of the very old – like tennis balls
tennis stars in tennis skirts are whacking

out beyond the courts, above the houses
and on towards the tennis in the sky,

like tennis balls that never die –
are shuddering.

## The Young

What they don't know is – the young, I mean –
that they, the young, will soon become the old:

where else, after all, have they come from?
Where else have these dreary people been?

## The Simple Fact

Being old is absolutely pointless.
All they do is get in people's way.

Can't they understand the simple fact
they need to *get a move on*? They so can.

## White Mice

Because of her white hair and bony knuckles
and tiny garden full of white birds

flying overhead with outstretched paws
and whiskers on their chins, and hairy tails,

she seems much older than she thinks she does
but, even if she is, it doesn't matter.

## Chocolate Biscuits

Being old's much easier than you think:
eat as many biscuits as you like

and let the children stuff themselves as well
and just *forgive everybody everything!*

## Sleepless Nights

The billionaire is haunted by his father
who also lay in bed and couldn't sleep;

who heard, or thought he heard,
the tramp of boots,

of thigh-length, highly polished, skin-tight boots,
approaching with a scythe across the lawn.

## The Horse

Lying on their chilly beds like luggage
waiting in the dark to be collected,

some are patient, some are less patient.
One old man is missing his horse.

## Like the Lost at Sea

The old, the old, stiffening in their sheets,
please can someone tell them what they're living for;

what the living – like the lost at sea,
hoping, and then losing hope – are living for.

## The Petite Housewife

She may be 'petite' but she's so violent
she likes to slash *other people's* wrists!

## The Ewe

She hasn't got a clue
where she's going

or, if she has,
she doesn't mind a bit;

she doesn't mind a bit
that growing old,

old and half-asleep,
is not her fault;

she doesn't mind a bit
about the abattoir,

she's sitting in his van
as good as gold.

## Chocolate-tipped Meringues

Why do women have to be so secretive?
(they look like they are doing what they're doing
but really they are doing something else!)
But being old means Jilly can't reach up

to hide the bars of chocolate-tipped
meringues
behind the things like porridge oats and rice.
Now she is obsessed by her feet.

## Rich and Famous

Rich and famous,
floating on his yacht,

just him
and his incontinence pad.

## The Residents

They dream,
like mutton chops on a plate

that dream of having once been lamb,
of youth.

They dream of youth
until the nurse bursts in.

They love the nurse.
She is so bright and breezy.

No more hunching over trays for her!
No more sulky staring into space!

They love the nurse.
Or if they don't they should.

## George

His eyes like drips of honey made by bees
that never liked the work in the first place

and certainly don't like the work now,
they're sick of it –

he blinks like a man
who's never going to figure out what's happening.

## The Billionairess

Her husband was a billionaire, apparently,
but, ancient as she was, she did a runner –

just her, the dog and the famous smile
that she can barely squeeze inside the caravan.

## Skin

He's sitting in his office with a coffee
examining the skin of the hands

that haven't been caressed
for a billion years.

## Smile, Smile, Smile

If you're old, remember not to cry,
remember to be very clean and neat;
that everything you feel like saying's boring,
and don't be fooled by nurses being nice,
they're actually *bored stiff* you're so boring.

What you have to do is smile, smile.
Remember not to cry
and smile, smile;
smile until nothing else makes sense
and everybody else can go to Hell.

## Woman in a Chair

Her feet and legs are big and soft like buns,
her breasts are in her lap. She is smiling.

*No,* she says, *she won't be having coffee.*
(It's not as if she wants to feel at home here!)

## The Tablecloth

When you're old,
you're old all the time,

you never get a break,
and it's embarrassing.

(Nobody must know he saw a rhino
balancing a teapot on its back.)

## The Elderly

First of all, they've got to be clean.
Secondly, they've got to be grateful.

And, thirdly, they have got to remember
that they are old and contribute nothing.

## Concrete in May

He sits in silence like the huge ashtray
made of concrete outside the hospital.

He doesn't want to think about the past.
He doesn't want to think about the future.

The only thing he knows is he knows
that this is what it's like being old.

## Ugly Shoes

Why do they always have to be so grumpy?
And wear such ugly shoes all the time?

Why? Because they're old, that's why,
and trying as hard as they can to refuse to get used to it.

## Happy Little Faces

It's true they can't stand up –
but they can swim
(if to bob about is to swim!).

Look at them,
their happy little faces
bob about like frogspawn in the spring.

## Does He Want to Reach a Ripe Old Age?

Does he want to reach a ripe old age?
to have some well-earned leisure? to reflect

on life and all its marvels?
He does not.

## Men in Winter

Have you noticed busy men are everywhere,
blowing leaves, fixing bicycles?

But one fine day they'll find that they prefer
staying in the house in the warm.

## Meeting the Vicar

I'm sorry but this dog is much too big,
she makes the little vicar look ridiculous,

she chugs along beside him like a sofa
being taken for its daily walk.

## Wilhelmina

They found her in the street with nothing on.
Imagine that! She must have looked amazing –
her clouds of frizzy hair, her rolls of fat...
Another time she walked into the lake.
It was snowing but she didn't care!
She found a cat floating in the rushes
and towed it back to land by its tail.

Things like that never bothered her.
She was still surprisingly strong
(physically, I mean). She used to say
she actually preferred being old.
I can still hear her saying merrily
*I can do whatever, now I'm old!*
which wasn't true, as it turned out.

## Pool

Those who are too old to walk
can float.

They smile as they float
like smiling weed.

## The Old Exist

The old must understand they are not young.
They cannot hope to be their friends:

the young
do not even know the old exist.

## What They Still Remember

They neither know nor care
that they forget

that what they still remember
never happened.

## Being Old Is Such a Waste of Time

A grumpy dog that farts, as if to say
*being old is such a waste of time*

some people find
is easy to relate to.

## Duck

The children –
who are certainly *not* children –
tell her what to do and what not to do
in such a nasty high-handed way

(as if they see no point in being nice
to someone who is old and can't eat
and follows them around like a duck
begging them to give it crusts of bread),

in such a nasty high-handed way
they make their mother cry –
either cry
or poke them with her handy little walking-stick.

## Cooking

Some of them really love cooking
and like to study all the latest cookery books

and all the new equipment and ingredients;
others feel sick if they cook.

## Spectacles

He settles down to read in his chair
and then remembers where he's left his spectacles.

He can either go downstairs and get them
or go to sleep and dream he's got them on.

## The Old Woman and the Young Man

The woman who would love to give him everything
(everything and more!)

but who can't,
dedicates her days to avoiding him.

## People Who Are Old Don't Have Fun

People who are old don't have fun,
or that's what people think, but they do –

they eat as many chocolates as they want
and go to sleep on the watery changing-room floor.

## These Furious Adults

These furious adults,
were they once his children?

And is it true
they've come to take him home?

## He Died the Way He Chose to Die

He died the way he chose to die and not
in someone's upstairs bedroom,
like an idiot,

with all the chocolates scattered on the floor:
he died at sea,
in his three-piece suit.

## People Who Are Old Are No Fun

People who are old are no fun.
*Whatsoever.*
All they do is moan.

(OK, OK,
I know I shouldn't generalise.)
All they ever do is moan, moan.

## Mothers

They come and go – how odd – without warning
and don't say much,
sometimes they say nothing,

and all the people who are old can do
is tell themselves their mothers used to love them,
and who's to say they did or they didn't,

and anyway it really doesn't matter,
or if it does
the ghosts should be more sensitive.

## The Warm Hot-water-bottle

People who are old don't like toast,
they don't like things to be too 'deep and meaningful'
and often they don't even like themselves;

they do their best, however, to be cheerful:
cheerfulness is like a warm hot-water-bottle
that everyone, however old, can share!

## What's the Point of Being Happy?

Because they're always trying to be happy
people who are sad
get exhausted –
and what's the point of being happy anyway?

Why not just be sad
and see what happens?
see if being happy's
overrated?

## People Who Are Old Can't Be Trusted

People who are old can't be trusted.
I know you want to trust them
but you mustn't:

people who are old are like women;
like sweetly smelling, unpredictable
strangers.

## Brassieres

When you're young
they make you look young
but when you're old
they make you look old.

## The Father of the Late Billionaire

He treats himself like an old man.
She forgets he *is* an old man.

## Success

His suicide was therefore a success,
success, that is, according to him –

the bronzed, bejewelled husband she abandoned,
taking with her the myopic dog.

## Debut Novels

If you're old, there is no further need
to read, far less critique, debut novels;

no need to go outside if it's raining,
or even if it's not; no need to knit;

no need to sleep; no need to wake up –
but do you need to use the loo? You do.

## You Can Ask for Anything You Want

You can ask for anything you want
and everyone is only too delighted

to have the chance to do something kind.
Being old is actually quite good!

## Mowing the Lawn

People who aren't old
have things to do

like mow the lawn
or go on holiday;

people who are old
do nothing.

## Spiders

Nobody notices at first
but every day the old are slowly shrinking.

They creep across the landings in their zimmer frames
like homesick spiders dressed in wool bootees.

## Old Ladies

Although they are old ladies,
and old ladies

terrify small children in their cots
and feed them cubes of sugar dipped in tea,

they do not necessarily
die painfully.

## The Old Man and His Dog

The old man and his dog
inch down the road
step by painful step
as if to say
*who will be the first*
*to be abandoned*
*and who will be the first*
*to pass away.*

## Awe

So being old's not all that it's cracked up to be –
The being rich and famous, hiring staff,

inspiring herds of callow youths with awe –
it's more about how awkward someone's staircase is.

## Being Trampled on by Labradors

We don't mind a bit,
on the contrary

we like the thought of being trampled on,
we like the thought of being old and squashed,

so old and squashed
we won't know whose our bodies are.

## The Woman Who Escaped

She looks as if she's never been outside,
as if she can't do anything but creep,

as if she's setting off to creep for ever
(in spite of wearing wool bootees for shoes).

## Arthur

He's not remotely interested in tea,
in anything, it seems, except himself,

a man who likes to rise in the morning
and spend the day in silence like snow.

## The Avenue

The dead escort the old, as if the old
were walking down an avenue of veils

that come up close then glide away again,
of restless and disconsolate veils.

## The Man Who Loved His Poodle

They find him on his bed, no longer conscious,
with Agatha sitting up beside him:

she sits completely still, like an owl
nobody knows how to comfort.

## Mrs X

Because she's got a hair on her chin
(or several hairs, if you look closer)
Mrs X resembles a parsnip,
a mild television-watching parsnip.

## Josephine

People who are old enjoy the company
of other people who are old, and cats.

One old man has got a snail, Josephine,
he keeps beside his pillow in a tank.

## Out Beyond the Cedars in Their Wheelchairs

They're parked beyond the cedars in their wheelchairs,
like cabbages in dresses wrapped in rugs,

cabbages that dream of being lollipops,
cabbages with hearts that can sing.

# ROOM 17

The sky does whatever the sky wants. Time has turned its back on the city.

YEVGENIA BELORUSETS

from *Lucky Breaks* by Yevgenia Belorusets
translated from the Russian by Eugene Ostashevsky

## The Grandmother Goes Shopping

If he thinks she loves him
he is wrong:

the moment he is out of sight, she buys herself
a pair of crimson heels on which to totter.

## A Grandmother Who Star-jumps

And here we have a grandmother who star-jumps.
She star-jumps every morning before breakfast,

before she hops onto her 3-speed bike
to battle with her grandsons again.

## The Grandmother Goes Swimming

I've never known a kangaroo to swim
but grandmothers? Of course they can. And do.

They swim until they're sick. Only joking!
They swim until their eyeballs fall out.

They swim until they're hanging upside-down
like upside-down kangaroos and elephants.

They swim until the water turns to amber
in which they are impaled like dead flies.

## The Grandmother and Her Granddaughters

The granddaughters
are glamping in the garden

in what she calls
The Hotel Palomino.

## The Grandmother in the Park

She walks straight past in nothing but her swimsuit
as if he was a bed of squashed campanulas.

## The Grandmother and Coco

The grandmother is breathing
like a rock

in order not to move
when Coco yaps.

## The Grandmother and Michelle at the Swimming Pool

He's watching from his chair
as if to say

Don't touch me now, Michelle,
touch me later.

## The Grandmother and Her Chocolates

If she eats five of them today
there'll only be three of them tomorrow

when she will be wishing she had eaten
four of them, not *five* of them, today.

## The Grandmother and the Rabbits

Her breasts are large and warm like two large rabbits
sitting side by side in the dark.

Her grandson puts his finger on their chins
to see if they're alive, and they are.

## The Grandmother and the Woman Next Door

When she says *Come in*
she means *Get out*

and when she says *Sit down*
she means *Die.*

## Grandmothers with Sweets

Some of them will give you sweets but others
have nasty little dogs on their laps

and some of them walk about smiling
(but when they smile it means they've got a headache).

## The Grandmother Relaxes

Like a pig,
if pigs don't feel the cold,

she likes to lie in ponds
not thinking pork.

## Grandmothers and Love

There's nothing they don't know about love!
The love of those who pray, of those who mourn,

the love of tempered strings for the bow,
of suicides in lidos for the sea.

## The Grandmother and the Visitor

It seems quite happy
so she lets it stay.

It watches her for hours
without moving,

occasionally tilting
its great horns.

## The Grandmother and the Chickens

And here she comes
running down the street

dodging trucks and clutching to her breast
chickens that have never heard of soup.

## The Grandmother and the Vertiginous Hillside

But now suppose a very bored grandmother
pushing her small grandson in his pushchair

down a vertiginous hillside
lets go.

## The Grandmother and Her Carnations

Earnest and alone,
she paints carnations

that smell not of carnations
but of turpentine.

## The Grandmother and Mr Tsitsipas

May all beings be at peace, especially
the troubled and mysterious Mr Tsitsipas;

may all beings be at peace, especially
bed-ridden ex-champions and their stets;

may all beings sleep in feather beds
and may they all be spoon-fed semolina.

## The Grandmother in the Afternoon

Her two large breasts (her two large fish!)
are bored.

As bored as two large fish that circle round
a tiny tank with neither weeds nor toys.

## The Grandmother and the Lion

She finds a lion lying on her bed
and asks if she can get him anything

but he just lies there looking very tired.
She tells him he can stay. And not to worry.

## The Grandmother in the Lake

What a lovely way
to be unbearable,

to stand and scream
like someone who can't swim.

## The Grandmother and Her Bike

Her breasts are large but her bra is small.
You can see it clearly through her dress

as, with a wave, she hops onto her bike
and disappears towards the doctor's surgery.

## The Grandmother and the Surgery

She's not afraid of him but of herself –
by which she means of what she might do,

by which she means she might do something rash,
by which she means something that betrays her.

## The Grandmother and Her Grandson

It simply isn't true that a grandson,
even one accustomed to disdain,

doesn't flinch. He flinches all the time.
And when he's with his grandmother he sobs.

## The Grandmother in Her Frilly Dress

Here she comes, in her frilly dress,
but look, there's something moving in her arms

and as he gets closer he sees blood
dripping from its paw onto her breast.

## The Grandmother and the Pool Attendant

It's only a matter of time before the grandmother
looks into the pool attendant's eyes

and tells him she would rather frolic there
than in the murky waters of his swimming pool.

## The Grandmother's Sofa

Here she comes,
fragile but determined,

to turf those fat Chihuahuas
off the sofa

for looking like they think they are
untouchable.

## The Grandson's Teeth

The grandson is lying through his teeth!
OK, she shouldn't say that, but he is –

or rather (which is worse) he is trying to
but all that ever happens is a *blush*.

## The Grandmother and Sky-diving

Is the hand that gives the pool attendant
golden thighs and eyes like sky the hand,

the hand she dreads, that dealt her
ugly feet?

## The Grandmother and the Tweed Coat

Although today's the hottest day so far,
today's the day that she decides to wear

her mother's and her grandmother's tweed coat
while painting fruit in direct sunlight.

## The Grandmother and the Rat

The grandson's got his hand down his trousers
in which his rat is trying not to laugh.

He waits for her to look the other way
then quickly tips it back into its cage –

or, not a cage,
it's more of a palace,

a palace for the dreams of bony orphans
who speak in words that have no written form.

## The Grandmother and a Member of the Public

A member of the public stops to look.
*Nothing serious, I hope,* he says.

Someone comes up and pushes in.
*Is she still alive?* The first man shrugs.

He doesn't understand that she's a hippo
sinking into unremitting mud.

## The Grandmother at the Station

And now the station-master kneels down
and whispers in her ear – but a train

rushes past as if to say *Forget it…*
It's tiring being hot all the time…

And now the station-master and the nurse
talk about each other's useless sons

one of whom's a swimming-pool attendant –
*as well as everything else!* says the nurse.

## The Grandmother and Her Visitors

At night
they sleep politely on the floor

but in the day
they sleep in her bed.

## The Grandmother in the Shower Room

Barely moving –
like a life-size croc

made entirely of chocolate
in a heatwave –

the grandmother is thinking to herself
*it couldn't have been him*

before collapsing
against the golden thighs of the pool attendant.

## The Grandmother's Birthday

The grandmother has got the perfect dog:
it's made of cake and it doesn't bark!

## The Grandmother in Bed

She loves to lie in bed
in the dark

thinking *thighs*.
She isn't thinking *rosary*.

## The Grandmother's Unbearable Mortification

The grandmother or, if not the grandmother,
somebody who looks like the grandmother,

is sitting in the middle of the road
and scratching at her groin as if to say

she's suffering, can't they see she's suffering
*unbearable mortification.*

## The Grandmother in the Middle of the Road

Somebody who looks like the grandmother –
the same short legs, the same ill-fitting dress –

is sitting in the road when a man
removes her dress with large hairy hands.

## The Grandmother's Hair

She feels the thick thigh of the doctor –
or could it be the swimming-pool attendant? –
hot against her hair

like a missionary
who feels the thick thigh of an elephant
while doing what has to be done.

## The Grandmother at the Pharmacy

The grandmother feels much younger
than many women who look half her age!

This woman on her phone, for example,
who looks at her distrustfully and leaves.

## The Grandmother's Knees

Children who have never seen a cow
are very sad, it's true,

but not as sad
as knees in jeggings that refuse to bend.

## The Grandmother Upstairs

She rests her head
against the doctor's thigh.

The doctor goes downstairs.
*Never mind.*

## The Grandmother in the Forest

Once upon a time there was a grandmother
who couldn't stop thinking about love

so late one night she walked into the forest
and begged the dark to give her a moose.

## The Grandmother and the Pears

The grandmother is slowly painting pears
and while she paints she eats a bar of chocolate

quickly,
before anyone comes.

## The Grandmother on the Bus

She's telling him what happened
in great detail.

*I'm very happy for you*, says the man,
looking closely at her large breasts.

## The Grandmother's Neck

When the driver presses his big face
hard against her neck like a bullock

she squeals with delight
but she shouldn't.

## The Grandmother and the Wives of Violent Men

The wives of violent men, the Pill, podiatry,
Holy Water, binders, certain tennis stars,

contraception, lack of contraception,
women in short shorts, bananas, necks,

and sofas piled high with bored Chihuahuas
are never to be mentioned by the sober.

## The Grandmother in a Sombrero

*There's no such thing as laziness*. The grandmother
is stationed on the lawn in a sombrero

observing now pears,
and now thighs.

## The Grandmother's Frock

If she couldn't wear her little frock
she thinks her life *wouldn't be worth living!*

(But then again
it's not worth living now.)

## The Grandmother and the Doctor's Thigh

She feels the doctor's thigh through his trousers –
his shin, his calf, his knee, his lean thigh –

which may or may not have been moisturised
and taken out to tan in the sun.

## The Grandmother's Shoes

Why has someone left some red shoes,
a yellow jug of pink and white carnations

and a peach on the kitchen table?
Plus a notice saying DO NOT TOUCH.

## The Grandmother's Smile

If she were to tell him
what has happened

he wouldn't understand
so when he goes

the grandmother
plans to smile normally.

## The Boredom of the Late Pool Attendant

The doctor is explaining to the grandmother
*not everyone likes thighs*. On the contrary,

you only have to bring to mind, he's saying,
the boredom of the late pool attendant.

## The Grandmother and Her Enormous Children

You can't expect a very small grandmother
to do what her enormous children do

which doesn't mean to say that it's OK
to come with sheets and gel and put her down!

## The Grandmother and the Murderers

Even athletes have, or have had, grandmothers,
even despots, billionaires and thieves

and those who fast, and those who sleep on rocks,
and large and small and medium-sized priests,

even they are grandsons. And the murderers?
The murderers are sweetest of them all.

## The Grandmother's New Home

Nobody must tell her where she is
and nobody must call, the woman says,
and nobody must say to the doctors
why not simply have her *put to sleep*.

## The Grandmother's New Friends

Drifting here and drifting there
in nighties
that fall apart
like slow-witted flowers,

they're never going to find
what they are looking for
because they have forgotten
who they are.

## The Grandmother and the Goose

*Touch me and I'll kill you*, says the goose
that stalks the gardens of the Grand Hotel.

The residents with whom she shares the dining-room,
smiling sweetly, say the same thing.

But they needn't worry! Someone tell them
she's really only interested in fruit.

## The Grandmother in Her Room

Those who visit her in her room
sometimes think they smell what smells like turpentine.

## The Grandmother and Her Apples

For reasons which she can't explain, the grandmother
has always found bowls of apples comforting

and when they come and take her paints away
the grandmother continues to observe them.

## The Grandson and the Doctor

But have you ever noticed,
says the grandson,

that when she talks she talks like a person
who's talking like a normal person talks?

## The Grandmother on the Lawn

Most afternoons she can be seen contentedly
sitting on the terrace watching fruit

but today she's lying on the lawn
because today she wants to be a poodle.

## Grandmothers' Chins

Women who are elderly,
like pigs,

have bristles on their chins,
and sometimes smile,

even if, inside,
they are sad.

## The Grandmother and the Counsellors

They understand those who wear slippers
and those who still totter on high heels

(or, OK, to be honest, those who *dream*
they're tottering along on high heels);

they understand the elderly are liars
and when they say *Don't touch* they mean *Don't look*.

## The Grandmother Paints Her Face

She paints her face, *she pulls herself together* –
but back in bed she can't forget she's doomed.

## The Grandmother Laughs

Oh yes, she says, and laughs, she still remembers
the golden shins and thighs of the attendant

as, bored and slow, he punched her yellow swimming-card
before returning to his warmed chair.

## The Grandmother at the Grand Hotel

The doctor calls the Home the *Grand Hotel*;
her daughters call it *Hotel Semolina*:

they totter here, they totter there, and, grudgingly,
they totter to the *Hotel Semolina* –

in which they find, smiling and undressed,
a mother with two breasts like two large fish.

## The Grandmother and Her Greetings Cards

Her room is very nice.
And please don't call.

And please don't send her cards.
(We've told the staff,

if anybody sends them,
to destroy them.)

## The Grandmother at Night

She's ringing for the nurses
who – she knows,

and who the nurses know –
will never please her.

## The Grandmother in the Flower Bed

She's standing in the flower bed
and waving.

Can't they understand
she is a dahlia?

## The Grandmother Enjoys Her Tea

Luckily for people with no teeth
somebody has invented custard.

## The Grandmother Goes for a Walk

Part of being old
is being slow;

the other part
is being even slower.

## The Grandmother's Bell

*May all beings be at peace* – but also
may all beings come when they are called!

And even if they don't (they 'can't be bothered')
may she never doubt the power of prayer.

## The Grandmother at Mealtimes

Dead and dying grandmothers prefer
not to be force-fed vanilla Complan

and even if they're neither dead nor dying
please can they not force-feed anyone else.

## The Grandmother and the Sound of Laughter

Every day he's somewhere
and he's laughing

and every day
she is somewhere else.

## The Grandmother and Erling Haaland

Have you ever seen a naked grandmother
swaying in a doorway late at night

and marvelled at the breasts that hang like cheeses
hanging in the shade in muslin bags?

She's on her knees. It's better not to look.
(But why be so aghast all the time?)

And now she's lying full-length in the corridor.
Her dressing-gown is nowhere to be seen.

And here comes Erling Haaland. And he's waving!
But adults can be so unpredictable.

Maybe he is waving not at her
but at the nurse that's on her way to kill her.

And now she sees, or thinks she sees, a tench.
The corridor is filling up with bilge.

The grandmother thinks she can't move –
which now of course we know to be true.

## Flocks of Sheep

On the day
she fails to wake up

flocks of sheep
beset Room 17

and fall apart
and understand nothing.

## The Grandmother Who Loved to Chat

She loved to chat so much, the little grandmother,
you'd even hear her chatting to her fruit

and she's still chatting now, but in a language
only the deceased can understand.

# MEN IN SHORTS

*For Amy*

*(in spite of the dogs)*

## Men

When a group of men in shorts runs by
we watch them run and then she turns and says
*There's more to life than men in shorts!*
But what?

## Springtime

Everything is suddenly bright green
and everyone out walking their dogs
is even more talkative than usual
and marvels at the glittering sea.

## The Woman with the Corgi

The woman with the corgi checks her watch.
She never stops checking her watch!
*I know,* she says, *I'd be lost without it.*
I reply *I like being lost.*

## Husbands

The English Bull Terrier called Toothpaste
is lying at her feet as good as gold.
She says her Toothpaste is a better friend
than they (she means her husbands) ever were.

## The Nice Cow

Today the Schnauzers' owner's looking cross
(almost as cross as his Schnauzers!):
and when I say *the cow's a nice cow!*
he looks at me as if he wants to strangle me
and bury me in concrete in a basement.

## The Neapolitan Mastiff

The woman with the Neapolitan Mastiff
we all adore is telling us that Mastiffs
*complement inadequate personalities.*
There's a slight pause as the rest of us
think of something tactful to say.

## Several Lovers

Here's the woman with the pug again.
She says her daughter's spoilt. And the pug.
She also says her husband is spoilt.
*Sitting on his fat arse all day!*
She says she's going to get herself a lover.
Or several lovers. And I wonder how.

## The Priest

I talk to him about his ordination
and what it must be like to be ordained
and as I talk I say to myself
*please stop talking now* but I don't.

## Brothers

I meet the skinny man with the Shih-Tzu
who tells me that The Will has now been read!
He said to the executor *I'm warning you,*
*I do not trust that dirty rat one bit!*
(By 'dirty rat' I think he means his brother.)
It starts to pour with rain. I say *Oh dear...*

## The Tall Policeman

*Because of you,* I say, *I now know*
*policemen are just normal human beings!*
The tall policeman whispers in my ear
*What I really like are cut flowers.*

## Nishikori

*Nishikori; servants of the curve;*
*hyenas on the plains of Ethiopia…*
when we stop and talk, the conversation
circles round us like another dog.

## Manliness

The Dachshund man grabs the ball and hurls it
far away towards the distant river
and when I say *That was very manly!*
he looks at me as if I've just said
the nicest thing I've said to him all summer,
no, the nicest thing he thinks I've ever said.

## The Letter

He sees she's got a letter in her hand
and says politely *Can I post that for you*;
after all, he passes the letter-box.
The lady says sadly *I don't trust you.*

## The Sea

He stops and looks approvingly at the sea
and shakes his head. *Calm as a mill-pond!*
But when I say I wonder why 'mill-pond'
he looks extremely irritated by me.

## The Tiny Reed Warbler

A tiny reed warbler has appeared,
as if from nowhere. How, we don't know.

## Drowning

This morning we are talking about drowning
and what the signals mean the lifeguards make
but when the Pomeranian starts barking
we talk about something else instead.

## Power-boats

We chat away – but we're always careful
never to upset anybody.
Take the power-boat owner, for example.
I talk about our dogs. Or the weather.
Distance runners. Hitting the wall.
But I never say I hate power-boats.

## Motherhood

The talk today's about having children
and about *not* having children.
Someone's saying not having children
makes a woman *very bad-tempered*.
I wonder if she herself…but no,
we like to keep it light, as I said.

## The Genius

In the end he had to give it up.
Genius is all very well
but genius is not enough, he says.
You've got to have *the right kind of temperament*.
We stand in silence in the long grass
considering our respective temperaments.

## Wild Flowers

We talk about protecting wild flowers.
He glares at them – *stupid wild flowers!* –
and I decide to spare him my new theory
about the *acrobatics of enlightenment*.

## A View of the Sea

We stand beside each other looking out.
I say *Tired?* He says *Not bad.*
Nothing moves. I say *Let me know.*

## Playing Cricket in the Mist

*'The wicket, sir, I can't see the wicket,*
he couldn't see the wicket, he was crying...'
And after asking if I want a butterscotch
he disappears into the mist again.

## Cathedral

Yes, he says, he's Welsh. Every week
for fifty years he sang in the cathedral.
But no, he says, he couldn't sing for me.

## What It's Like to Ride a Cow

You ask me what we talk about. Whatever.
Men in shorts. Jesus in shorts.
What it's like to ride a cow. But mostly
everyone just talks about their dogs.

## The Flautist

He's waiting to collect his son from school.
He doesn't know the area, he says.
He says he's just recently divorced.
(How recently is recently, I wonder.)
Asks me what I do. I don't answer.
Then I say How about you?
He says he is a flautist. A flautist?
I can't come up with anything to say.
I wonder what his ex is doing now
and concentrate my mind on the 'a'.

## Huskies

She says a husky *even smells different.*
I'm watching her. She needs to calm down.

## What My Mother Said

My mother always said the clothes I wear
should not attract attention *as clothes.*

## Jealousy

My nephew in his wheelchair gets jealous
of people who still manage to stand up!
The people I am jealous of are people
who manage to locate well-fitting bras.

## Dentistry

The couple with the Mastiff explain
their daughter and their son are both dentists.
I try and change the subject but, no,
everyone starts talking about dentistry.

## The Beard

The man with the Saluki loves dogs!
He left the Chow at home. *It's the weather.*
I can think of nothing but his beard.
I'm thinking *Does it have to be so long?*

## Little Rabbits

The blood-stained lurcher likes little rabbits;
his master and myself prefer ice cream.

## BBQ

He's asking everybody, not just me,
anyone he knows with a dog,
*bring the dogs*, he says, *don't be shy*,
but nevertheless I am shy unfortunately.

## The Tubby Whippets

When she says they're getting rather tubby
the whippets' owner whispers *So are you*.
She jabs her finger at him and pronounces him
*the rudest man she has ever met!*

## Rain

It's raining and a group of us are sheltering
underneath the sycamore tree.
The man who breeds Chihuahuas says unhappily
I think about chocolate day and night.

## The Terrible Mess

We talk about *the terrible mess*
they left behind. (Didn't we all?)

## Fathers

Fathers. It keeps coming back to fathers.
No, she says, she'll never forgive him!
I keep my little mouth shut about mine.

## Running

We're talking about running again
when suddenly he mentions his wife.
And then he says *Sorrow is bliss*.
And I refuse to let the man go
until he tells me what he means by that.

## Love

Today, to my surprise, the poodle man
tells me he's in love! At eighty-three!
And then he tells the car-park attendant
and then the woman with the Basset Hound.
The woman with the Basset Hound ignores him.

## The Mysterious Man

A man appears with three obnoxious elephants
(that's what he keeps calling them – his elephants!),
ties a wire-haired Dachshund to a tree
and disappears into the dark woods.
The three obnoxious elephants turn round
and walk – or rather waddle – back to somewhere
where they can get a decent cup of coffee.

## Visitors

*Don't you find they seem to eat so much?*
*Yes*, we all agree, *they eat so much!*

## The Woman with the Lab

The woman with the Lab takes my arm.
She starts to cry. She whispers *Please don't go.*

## Cows

As usual, it is all about the cows.
She's saying if you don't bother *them*
*they* won't bother *you* and I agree.
We think how nice it is to agree.

## Our Plans for Today

Somebody suggests we write them down
and put them in a hat – so, for example,
I might get to cook for someone's mum
and he might have to fumigate my ants.

## The Man from Cheshire

When someone comes along I don't recognise
my neighbour says she thinks he's from Cheshire.
She pauses while I take this fact in
then adds *But I've got nothing against Cheshire!*

## The Word Mistress

The doctor passes with a different dog.
Then I see he's with a different woman.
I know it is more tactful to refrain
from saying the word mistress so I don't.

## The Musician

When he says Jazz I say *Jazz?*
*Jazz is my idea of a NIGHTMARE!*
which is such a stupid thing to say
to someone who's a serious musician.

## The Adorable Man

The man with the adorable Spinone
(and yes, the man's adorable too)
asks me for a coffee. I decline.
He says *Oh never mind!* But I do mind.

## Summertime

The cows are standing calmly in the river.
They seem to be in a sort of trance.
Everyone who comes along is smiling.
*Perfect! Not a cloud in the sky!*

# BONKERS

## The Afghan Hound

Go, he's shouting, *go*, but she just sits there
looking down her nose at the Labradors

who bounce around the beach with open mouths
the colour of raspberry coulis and rusting engine-parts.

## The Basset Griffon Vendeens

When their owner finally 'makes tracks'
she says she needs – or 'is in need of' – chocolate

(and I refrain from telling her the bed
my mother lived and died in was full of it).

## The Basset Hound

Because he's 'got a meeting to go to'
he drags the Basset off to the car,

throws him in the back and pulls away.
'A meeting with a lady!' says the poodle owner.

## The Bichon Frise

He's like a little hairdo on legs
nobody must touch or get wet

and when the little hairdo pirouettes
the little hairdo gets some brie or duck.

## The Boxer

He scatters toddlers left, right and centre
and tramples on their toys as if he owns the place

and all the owner does is say *I'm happy*
*as long as he is happy!* And he is.

## The Bulldog

The scabby Bulldog squats
and she unclips him

and walks the other way
to a life

in which to be alone
with her shower gel.

## The Cavalier King Charles Spaniel

He never stops smiling – like a man
banished yet again from the kitchen

of somebody he calls 'a single lady'
whose Cavalier King Charles he can't stand.

## The Chow

The bony woman with the fluffy Chow
is standing in the rain like a heron

establishing itself as a murderer
hour after shimmering hour.

## The Chihuahua

A silver-haired gentleman in swimming trunks
is feeding his Chihuahua grains of sugar

and when he gets bored he gets up
and rinses his fingers in the sea.

## The Cocker Spaniel

Although the bouncy Cocker's up for anything,
her owner looks so painfully shy

everyone's reluctant to initiate
anything as bold as conversation.

## The Collie

The Collie has got work to do. He can't
sit around all day being stroked

by women in creased trousers in whose pockets
ancient Smackeroos turn to dust.

## Corgis

The Corgis are his daughter-in-law's Corgis.
He says he'll never feel at home again.

## The Dachshunds

All they ever want to do is bite
but all their mistress ever lets them do

is *trundle, trundle, trundle* straight ahead
as if they are sedated or on wheels.

## The English Bull Terrier

This naked-looking English Bull Terrier
may be almost blind but she is happy

because this is the perfect day for wallowing
in the shallows of a warm sea.

## The German Shepherd

The woman with the limp's German Shepherd
is getting more and more disobedient

and when she goes to hospital there's nobody
who wants to look after him for her.

## The German Short-haired Pointer

Telling me his Pointer's so *untrainable*
he keeps it in a cage in the outhouse,

he glares at her – as they glared at me
for failing to achieve the perfect ponytail.

## The German Wire-haired Pointer

The woman with the German Wire-haired Pointer –
who someone else was taking for a walk,

a man in shorts who said he was her brother –
referred to him today as her husband.

## The Gordon Setters

The Gordon Setters can't believe their luck!
Their owners, on the other hand, who neither

race across the golden sands nor slobber,
stand beside their cars and despair.

## The Great Dane

A man in black is leading a Great Dane
along the promenade towards the Bowling Green

and every now and then he stops and folds
her loops of drool into a handkerchief.

## The Hungarian Vizsla

The man with the Hungarian Vizsla
joins me in the shelter of the shed

and side by side we stare at the rain
and wonder what the other one is thinking.

## The Irish Wolfhounds

We whisper in the dark like teenage moths
of Panama, Bolivia, Brazil…

nobody can hear us but the dogs,
fast asleep in their reflective harnesses.

## The Jack Russell Terriers

The owners of the dogs who chase tennis-balls
avoid the owners of the dogs who don't

because they know that all of them are thinking
*there must be more to life than throwing tennis-balls.*

## The Kerry Blue

The man whose Kerry Blue is being sick
(it's actually his wife's) says their fridge

is always crammed with raw defrosting chicken-thighs
he says he thought at first were for him.

## The Lurcher

Rubber bones are squeaking in the mist
as everyone waves madly to their dogs –

everyone that is except the man
whose lurcher's only interested in cricket.

## The Mastiff

The widow with the evil-looking Mastiff
feeds her beef in wafer-thin slices

that tremble like the body of Christ
the priest would place like snowflakes on my tongue.

## The Miniature Poodles

The wedding-cake was grey to look like rubber
and all the little bridesmaids were poodles

(and obviously I didn't like to say
what fun it sounded yet how sinister).

## The Patterdale

The woman with the hyperactive Patterdale
hurls the rubber ball across the sand

while stubbornly maintaining the expression
of PE teachers during school concerts.

## The Pomeranian

The owner of the dog who's 'getting worse'
kisses its pyjamas and it growls.

## The Rhodesian Ridgeback

The mission of a tick is to suck –
*like poetry itself!* – the dentist says –

as much of someone's blood as it can.
His Ridgeback's armpits are like sows, he says.

## The Saluki

His purple hood so big it hides his face,
the man who walks the millionaire's Saluki

doesn't really 'walk it' – he just sits there
getting stoned on a large rock.

## The Scottish Terrier

I'm not the only person to have noticed
how much the handsome builder of the boatshed

seems to like the woman with the Scottie.
And also she, him. But it's irrelevant.

## The Setters

A woman dressed in tweed with several Setters,
a whistle on a lanyard round her neck,

is holding forth about her dog's diet.
She looks at us sternly. *Raw mink.*

## The Sheltie

The little Sheltie runs into the sea
and snaps at it as if it were a fly,

or millions of flies, made of water,
who've got no legs and don't know what to do.

## The Shih Tzus

The owners of the Shih Tzus – men in suits
who've spent the last two hours on the beach

meekly chasing after them with sausage slices –
deny their dogs are getting on their nerves.

## The Springer Spaniel

A woman with a Springer and a poo bag
disappears into the paper shop,

having lost the rubber lamb chop
the dog from down the road is running home with.

## The Standard Poodle

Although it's true the Poodle's old and grey
she steps towards us like a ballerina

stepping primly out onto a stage –
or half a ballerina, half a chicken.

## The Stray

The little one-eared dog that long ago
someone found tied up beside a motorway

and carried home has come to the conclusion
*the only thing worth living for is rats.*

## The Weimaraner

The Weimaraner stares at the moon
as if to say the girly Pekingeses,

having been denied even brief
*experiences of awe*, are beneath him.

## The West Highland Whites

Suddenly a dozen dazzling Westies
come skidding down the steps to the beach,

followed by a man in slides who's shouting
*I'm going to strangle you in a minute!*

## The Whippet

The Whippet owner is in constant pain
and flinches as he turns towards the rocks

and limps away... like the lame nun
who locked me up and never came back.

## The Yorkshire Terrier

A woman wearing patent leather boots
totters round the corner with a Yorkie

she snatches up when she sees the ocean
as if to say *she wants to go home.*

# UNTIL THE TEARS ROLL DOWN MY CHEEKS LIKE HONEY

## The One-legged Man

On a wind-swept hill a one-legged man
walks towards a woman in a bobble-hat.
They greet each other.
In the middle distance,
something white that could be a sheep.

## Birdsong

I like the way we only meet outside,
and only ever talk about dogs;

I like the way the woods and sheep seem painted,
with painted trees, and pre-recorded birdsong

(he doesn't notice things like real birds –
which seems to have endeared him to me, oddly);

I like the way I'm having fun inventing
the woman I'm inventing to befriend him.

## His Dusty Jacket and His Ice-cold Hands

I almost think I nearly want to touch him,
no, to touch not him, to touch his jacket,
his dusty jacket and his ice-cold hands;
I can't imagine what his house is like,
his work, his phone, his friends, none of that;
he's like an actor with a walk-on part
who walks on limping, shivers, and walks off.
Anyway it's cold. We can't stay long.
Underfoot the blades of grass are frosty.
We need to hurry back to where we're from.
I wonder what his friends think he's like,
how his friends and family would describe him.
And does he even have any friends?
Am I his friend? No, I'm an *acquaintance*.
And what about brothers and sisters?
Does he have 'loved ones'? And do I?
Yes, I do. But I don't mention them.

## Being Looked at by a Man Standing Very Close Beside Me

Being looked at feels like being squeezed,
being squeezed so tight I can't move.

I try to shut my eyes but I'm so terrified
even my eyelids won't move.

## The Tall Giraffe

He doesn't cook.
He's got a cough. ('It's nothing.')
He's got no name.
His trousers are too thin.
Or maybe he has got *too many* names.

I don't know if the dogs are his or not.
Or even if he likes them particularly.
Hard to tell. And does he like *me*?
And does he ever wonder what I'm thinking?
Does he think I'm thinking about *him*?

However close we get to someone else
we can never know what someone's thinking.
They might as well not even be there even,
or sealed in a case like an exhibit –
a dusty head-dress or a stuffed giraffe.

## The Mystery of My Submission

I love his self-effacing, hangdog look!
I don't know why I do but I do.
I don't know why it doesn't make me think
*he's boring* and *I'm going* but it doesn't.

## Menswear

Let's talk about quantum foam, and menswear,
let's talk about myopia, utopia,
rosehip syrup, rosehip oil, anything
in order not to have to share the silence
of being in the silence on our own.

## Please Can He Not Know a Thing about Me

Please can he not know where I live
and please can he not know where I work

and please can he not know and not suspect
my cowardice, my vanity, my rage.

Rage? What rage?
The rage of being meek,

of talking like I think I ought to talk
and smiling like I think I ought to smile.

## What Other People Think

Other people think of him as flawed.
After all, he's only got one leg.

However, he knows certain things we don't:
how to not need duplicate legs;

how to be tight-lipped and level-headed;
how to live without having died.

## Sitting on the Bench like a Snail

I'm sitting on the bench like a snail
sitting on a grave in the rain.
He isn't going to come.
There's no point waiting.
It's probably best if I go.
And even if he does appear suddenly
I'll go at once, before I never go,
before he's choked by things I shouldn't say,
by pig snouts, goose feet, maggots, blood-stained poodles.

## Jesus and the Radios

If Jesus can wear jeans
and mend radios,

the long-haired, one-legged man
can make me sing.

## Two Strangers in a Field with Some Sheep

Not only did we meet but he talked to me,
as if he knows I like it when he talks to me,
as if we're not two strangers any more
but, in a way, I like it when we are

and how he doesn't know what my name is.
And he must have a name himself.
But anyhow
I don't know what it is and I don't want to know.

## My Private Life

I'm here because out here I'm never shouted at.
On the contrary, I am spoken to
by a man who can no more shout
than an unexcited hedgehog can.

But what do I know? Maybe he's been shouting
all day long, until his throat is raw,
and now he's come out here to re-charge
in order to go back and shout some more.

## It Hasn't Stopped Raining for Days

It hasn't stopped for days so no wonder
I haven't seen him.
Nobody has.
Or maybe he is ill.
I'll send him roses!
(Babies in a smithy. Or Nijinsky
dancing with a tapir or a moose.
Yes, he's like a moose – as big, as shy,
as bored by bunches of expensive roses.)

## Please Don't Answer *Chess*

Athletics? Ballet? Please don't answer *chess*!
Please don't be embarrassed. Please go home.
Please go somewhere else. Take a seat.
Please forgive me if I don't know where.
Every body marvels at contortionists.
Please don't speak unless you're spoken to.
And don't forget to *never know my name.*
And please have pity on the champion.
Observe his psychological collapse.

## Alone with Me

Please don't let it not be true he's here
in order to forget about his radios;

in order to spend time alone with me.
Please don't let him want to start avoiding me.

## The Golden Lion

Thirteen days since we last met.
Same old jacket. Same old grumpy face.
He's been in town. Came back yesterday.
I thought I heard him say he's seen a lion –
but I couldn't have. I heard him say
he walked into the park and met a lion.
And put his arms round the lion's neck.
I thought I heard him say he *wrapped* his arms
round the lion's neck but I couldn't have.
The lion's neck is thick and its fur
is warm and golden like the dunes that men,
arriving at the shores of love,
sink into.

## I Need a Haircut and I Need It Now

I want to ask him so many questions –
but I know I mustn't so instead

I duck behind the hedge and rip my earrings out
because they keep catching in my hair.

## The Hide-out in the Mountains

It's like it isn't him that smiles the smile,
the smile is deployed to smile him:
his face is like a hide-out in the mountains
suddenly being strafed by light.

## Between the Devil and the Deep Blue Sea

If hope's his Devil,
I'm his Deep Blue Sea.

## Never Mention Mother

Maybe he's just bored to tears, like: Please,
I couldn't care less about Kafka
and Kafka's mice. And *never mention Mother.*

## Bobby Fischer's Eyes

His eyes, like Bobby Fischer's, glitter dangerously.
I wonder what he thinks of as his home.

## The Sun Will Rise Tomorrow

His jacket may look warm but it's not.
She promised they were juicy but they weren't.

His father said he did but he didn't.
The sun will rise tomorrow. *No it won't.*

## It's Possible to Walk in the Countryside

It's possible to walk in the countryside
with only one leg but it's not easy.

The sites of amputees' amputations
are never to be seen or even thought about.

Amputees can sometimes be pig-headed.
I myself am thinking *baked apple*.

## A Visit to the Grave of the Dancer

When he says his trousers are too thin,
the fields are too muddy, or he drinks too much,
when he fails to wonder at the countryside
and grumbles at the weather, at the dogs –
and *what's Milena got to do with anything?* –

I don't mind a bit; on the contrary,
for me it's fun to try and raise a smile:
it leaps up like a boy released from school
or, no, a dancer risen from the dead
who shakes his golden tresses free of worms.

## A Snowy Afternoon in December

Who is it who says he is too cold?
And who is it who turns and says goodbye?

And who is it who'd rather die than tell him
that when she says goodbye she means hello?

## A Slice of Cake Wrapped in Silverfoil

I can't believe his woebegone look
hasn't made me grab him by the shoulders
and give him a good shake long ago
but here I am giving him cake!

## Everything About Him

Everything about him. For example,
he seems to love hotels; he can't sing;
he knows the names of hundreds of makes of racing cars;
he doesn't see the point of being cold;
he's upright, clean, tight-lipped and unexcitable,
like hardened toothpaste in a hardened tube.

And lots of things that I do he'd pooh-pooh:
my curtain-hooks take over my life;
I scrunch my hair like the hair of an ageing rock star;
I think too much – all night! – like child acrobats
training underground, in tears, by candle-light;
I talk too much; and when I swim, I swim too much,
and as I take my leave I apologise,
standing on a rock,
to the waterfall.

## Angry Golfers, Sinister Children

Angry golfers, sinister children,
floral dresses, tailless cats,
musophobes, remorse... I talk too much...

He sinks onto the bench... When he dies
I'll leave a little posy on his grave
for him and for the old-fashioned snails.

## St Catherine of Siena and Her Ring

Do saints like riding horses?
Do they swim?
Do saints have dogs?
Dogs help you not despair –
you have to try and be the sort of person
you think your dog expects you to be!
(Or maybe saints have got their gods for that.)
Anyhow he's gone, and I am angry,
angry with myself for having hoped.
(I wonder if St Catherine of Siena
ever felt like this and if the ring
fashioned from Christ's foreskin
helped at all.)

## My Big Worry

Avoiding me?
Of course he's not avoiding me.
He never even saw me in the first place!

(By 'saw'
I mean he saw and he didn't see:
it's not as if I'm one of his radios!)

## *Everybody Loves Me*

My only hope's to understand the ostrich.
To do exactly what the ostrich does.
Which is what? Repeat to herself
*Everybody loves me* and shimmer.

## So Woebegone, So Flabby, So Alone

I'm thinking *Does he have to be so flabby?* –
so woebegone and flabby and alone –

alone except for two indignant crutches
that wish they didn't have to mind a leg.

## The Smile, When It Comes...

The smile, when it comes, comes out of nowhere:
as if he's paid an old, bejewelled hippogriff
to come out of his cave and say hello.

## A Jumble of Old Radios

Because he says his hobby's *mending radios*
I'm trying to say something about radios –

but what I really want to do is ask him
to carry me, like the sky the lark.

## My Controversial Theory about Bobby Fischer

The film he watched last night was so boring
he nearly turned it off. (Then why didn't he?)
No, he can't remember the name.
Tomorrow I will ask about sport:
does he watch sport? (Or 'follow sport'?
Does 'follow sport' sound better?) I won't mention
my controversial theory about Bobby Fischer.

## The Aeroplane

The fact that he's not here
is like an aeroplane

fallen from the sky
and non-negotiable.

## The Disappearing Mouse

The very first smile I saw him smile
ran across his face like a mouse
that disappeared as quickly as it came;
as if we both agreed it never happened.

## Fantasy Involving a Hairbrush

Fantasy:
I'm sitting on the bench

and he's beside me
brushing my hair.

## How to Share a Banana

Please sit down, relax, enjoy the sunshine,
and please don't talk if talking feels wrong;
please don't take your coat off; take no notice
every time I start and then stop,
please don't bother; always get my name wrong;
please don't move; tell me everything;
please don't tell me if it's all too much,
please stand up, please sit down, please go,
please don't be as stubborn as I think you are,
please be good at chess; please don't go,
please don't be afraid to stand up,
to walk away without a second thought,
to go to Hell without a star to guide you,
without a choir that never stops its squeaking;
please don't smile if you don't want to;
please accept a piece of my banana
and please don't be afraid to sit still.
Rival the serenity of Spassky.
And please don't be afraid to be afraid
and please don't be afraid to sit still
and why not eat a piece of my banana
all the way from Ecuador, why Ecuador?
tell you later, later never comes,
please don't glue the pieces to the board.
Do saints cook? Do they like swimming?
Do they own, or ever want to, dogs?
Are dormice mice? Don't eat internal organs.
Please don't crush the snails: crush the rain.
Crush the raindrops down inside my neck.
Tell me if it's true and please believe me
when I say *I don't believe a word.*
Please don't answer. Please don't smile. *Deadpan.*
Please don't touch me if you don't want to.
Please sit down and don't say a word.

## A Boring Man

Can someone tell me how to stop the stranger
becoming a boring man I now know?

## A Man and a Woman on a Bench

He sits beside me trying not to cry,
regardless of how many legs he's got.

## Please Don't Be Afraid to Meet My Eye

Please don't be afraid to come near;
please don't be afraid to touch my hair;

please don't be afraid to grip my neck,
to squeeze until the tears roll down like honey;

please don't stop until I tell you to,
please don't stop until my blood runs cold.

## The Man Who Didn't Sleep

He said he didn't sleep.
I didn't ask.
But I can just imagine him in bed –
quivering, and begging for a cat.

## The Man Is Gone

The man is gone
but in my dreams he's back:

he swings his unincinerated leg
and waves his unincinerated arms

and tells me it's OK
and I believe him.

## Dachshunds

There's more to life than trying not to cough,
there's more to life than greeting total strangers,
there's more to life than golf, than going faster;
there's more to life than Dachshunds and hotels;
there's more to life than sharing a banana;
than hope,
than loss of hope,
than Bobby Fischer;
there's more to life than hyperactive mice,
than mud,
than men,
than trying not to cry;
than bandages and crutches and insomnia;
than men with unrefrigerated legs.

## The Day He Took His Jacket Off

Put the jacket on again please
so we can be like how we were before

when it was like a meeting with a jacket,
not a meeting with an actual man.

## Outside the Golf Club Car Park on a Windy Day

The angry golfers bite their purple lips.
Outside the gate my amputated stranger
watches me approach but doesn't wave.

Waving's something other people do,
most of whom don't need to lean on gates
and none of whom is him, or is more loveable.

## Kafka's Fear of Mice

Please come here at once and brush my hair.
Please can I discreetly take you home.
Are you what I hope you are or not?
That's what I am trying to find out.
In a way, you're like a lost sheep.
If you want to bleat, then please bleat.
Lying down is not for the faint-hearted.
Bedrooms can be overrun by mice.
Mice can be unclean and uncontrollable
and often are. *They bite you on the lips.*
I haven't got all day. (Oh yes she has.)
Certain things I can't really say.
In a way you're like a lost mouse.
Feel free to squeak if you want to.
It's hard for me to know what to say.
*I want you to be someone I don't know.*
Please can I be told to sit still.
Not everyone likes mice. Look at Kafka.
Kafka couldn't sleep because of mice.
Please can I go home to my mother.
It would mean so much to me.
She's dead.

# THE SURLY MOTHERS OF SUCCESSFUL MEN

## short pieces of memoir

## The Bungalow (1)

On the beach below, unruly children dart about the sand like little birds while at the underrated cliff-top care home the residents are being wheeled outside.

## Palazzo Trousers

It's no good him wishing I'm the sort of woman whose white palazzo trousers are always as clean as a whistle because I'm not.

## Ants (1)

They're marching off to found a new colony where, one, there's no such thing as having fun and, two, there's no such thing as being loved, while on their dusty ledge above my bed the spiders cram their tiny mouths with flies.

## My Uncle's Private Parts

He let me walk beside him to the village but on the way he ducked behind a hedge and told me *not to move* but I followed him and that was when I saw what I saw for the first time, and my uncle never let me walk with him again.

## My Mother-in-Law Comes to Tea

She gazes at my garden then comments *The trouble is one has to be so patient.*

## The Boulder

The granite boulder dominates the valley where, far below, a woman made of flour falls apart in her flour cottage.

## Culottes

He wants to say how lovely she is looking but today she's wearing the culottes.

## The Leg of the One-legged Jockey

The one-legged jockey wants another leg, the businessman wants some mayonnaise, and what I want is a pair of Japanese Hokas.

## Father (1)

He called me *wilful, rude* and *disobedient* or would have done had he not been busy.

## The Man in Pyjamas

Dressed in old pyjamas and brown shoes, he shuffles through the yard and starts complaining, but nobody can *force* his wife to love him, even if he does give her chocolate.

## Wedding Day

I thought it was a hair in my mouth but it was two thin crane-flies getting married.

## Fountains

They can simply turn and walk away back to their remote and sunlit villages, if they have remote and sunlit villages, with fountains, and forget all about me.

## Foible

Groin, moist, soiled, oiled, hoick.

## The Woman in the Purple Trousers

The woman walking past in purple trousers looks exactly like my late sister, she's walking stiffly past on bony legs, I'm sorry but she's like a bony turkey, should I stop her? What should I say? *I like your purple trousers? Are you dead?*

## Walking Backwards

When I was a child and walked backwards, he would say *You're acting like a child.*

## The Visitor Regards My Big Black Dog

Visitor: We definitely wanted a *small* dog. Bigger dogs just get in the way! And my partner says she really dislikes *black* dogs. I'm the same. They're kind of *depressing*!

## The Surly Mothers of Successful Men (1)

Which surly mothers? What successful men?

## The Dirty Look

He tells the other man I can't drive, and the other man gives me a dirty look, as if to say *That's where I draw the line!*

## The Electricity Sub-station

It's all very well him calling it an electricity sub-station but what *is* an electricity sub-station? A place where tiny passengers change trains? It sometimes makes a melancholy humming noise as if it wants them all to go back home.

## What to Teach Your Children

Leave the house, alone, every morning, wearing dark glasses; in your hand a cup of coffee, even if it's cold. Teach this to your children. Punish them.

## The Little Stone

Noticing the little stone the size of a walnut that I had noticed several days before, I found, to my surprise, I had grown fond of it.

## The Man with Undyed Hair

I refuse to be in love with anyone except the man with undyed hair he used to be.

## The Other Person

The way in which I'm always over here and the other person's always over there.

## Ears

Do you ever get the uncomfortable feeling your life is being lived by someone else who people seem to need to think is you? How do you hide a surfboard? Are there chickens making themselves at home on your sofa? And do you long for perfectly formed ears?

## The Wounds of Successful Men

Never disrespect the wounds of successful men.

## Heatwave

My sister, as usual, is getting on my nerves. She is wearing nothing but a pair of underpants and keeps on trying to catch me up and suddenly I spin around and push her in the nettles.

## The Leftover Sausages

I don't want to eat them and I don't want to throw them away. If only they were apricots in syrup.

## Buckinghamshire

My sister was reprimanded for writing Bucks, and not Buckinghamshire, in full, but I don't mind how many times I write Buckinghamshire in full.

## Roger Federer in Switzerland

One of sport's undisputed geniuses, here he is hitting in the snow, snowflakes falling steadily like lilies Kierkegaard tells us fall like joy. (I think he means the joy of being silent, he says we are unable to be silent.)

## Question (1)

But if I want to forget whatever it was, why do I write it down, I'd like to know?

## The Visit to the Care Home

She wants to, but it's not because she wants to, it's just because she knows she *will have* wanted to, if she doesn't, so she says she wants to.

## Uncles

I prefer the ones who have died; the ones who are alive are old, like gods. At Christmas the married ones send shortbread. One of them owns a giraffe.

## The Doctor's Question I Found So Hard to Answer

And what difference does it make if you think your sister *died by accident* or *on purpose*?

## Women with Straight Hair

My fear of women with straight hair's not fear, it's more like *awe*, plus a sort of pity.

## Bathmat

Bored to tears, it looks at me and thinks, Why not make her slip and bang her head and lie, forgotten, on the cold, wet floor?

## Bodies in the Snow

Is wool fur or hair? or not? and why? And is it only poodles who have pom-poms, they tend to get problems with their ears, you need an oiled cotton-bud ideally, their feet are small and dainty like a pig's, but I prefer a dog with paws like bears', I used to have a beautiful St Bernard, as a child I couldn't sleep without him, he'd tell me all these stories about Switzerland – bodies in the snow, depraved philosophers, mountains like pistachio ice cream. I'd cuddle up beside him in the dark although I knew quite well he wasn't there.

## The Things He Says

Not only the things he says but the things he doesn't say.

## The Holiday

I arrive too early, paddle too far out, wash my clothes by hand like a peasant; I slice the organic zucchini the wrong way, I think too much, there's not enough butter.

## The Residents

They huddle in their corners spilling tea, too weak to rise, too weak to punch the visitors, to snatch their fruit and hurl it in their faces; no, they can't do anything except fold their little hands in their laps, hands as soft as eyelids gnawed by snails.

## Gentleness

Grief is understandable but this, being hurt by someone gentle, less so.

## The Letter H

The little H is like a naughty aphid tucked inside the phlox of the Lord.

## Salt

I'm not exactly blaming the curtains but hour after hour I'd lie awake, haunted, I can't help it, by the woman curled up on the floor in the flat where no one was allowed to touch the curtains, day or night, they had to be kept shut; haunted by the woman I tormented by pouring salt down her bright-red throat the way the hairless nuns poured salt down mine.

## My Uncle's Cooking

What about the man who called me 'svelte' – and as you know I am not svelte – and I was so embarrassed all I said was, 'What's the etymology of *that*?'; who, when he saw me coming round the corner (I can't believe I'm saying this) waved and made my heart give a sort of flutter, tiny, but a flutter nonetheless, and I could tell you now in every detail what we stood there in the mud and talked about, we talked about Hayne's manuals, garden gates, how he uses fungi for kindling; humility; divine retribution, *hope as patience with the light turned on* or did he say *with the light left on* or simply *with the light on*, I'm not sure, and as he spoke I watched the chocolate mud turn his shoes, sinking in the ruts, the colour of my uncle's *poires Hélène*, and then he said something like that God's *the presence of His own ideas in us*, or did he say *our own ideas in Him*, anyway I think I'm trying to say, or trying to somehow stop myself from saying, I'm much less unromantic than I think I am, and why the French, or German, or whatever? Why start speaking *German* all of a sudden?

## The Sister Who Didn't Exist

The first, if not the only, man who loved me had a sister, I discovered later, he'd banished from the world we were inventing.

## Mouth

Because my mouth is mine I feed it tapenade and spoonfuls of raspberry jam and raspberry jelly.

## The Bungalow (2)

In the cliff-top bungalow a woman is reading a book of short stories in which a woman in a bungalow is reading a book called *The Bungalow.*

## The Doctor's Hands

Although the doctor's eyes are warm and tender, the doctor's hands are like a bunch of fish. I wonder if he plays a musical instrument and, if he does, does he play *wholeheartedly*?

## Lip Balm

But when she tries to tell him the truth, he bridles, like a man who's being kissed by lips that have been sprinkled with glass splinters, or not so much sprinkled with as smeared with, splinters she's embedded in her lip balm.

## Girls Who Disobey

Girls who disobey have it easy, girls who disobey have unbrushed hair, they eat until they're sick, they hiss like geese forever being told *not to honk*, who leave the valley early, just like that; girls who disobey are hard to come by; girls who disobey live lives like kings', the sanity of billions at their fingertips, they murder, murder, to their hearts' content, while far below the footmen whisper *No, don't let this be happening* but it is, girls like us deny ourselves nothing.

## Pineapple Shampoo

He'd shut me in a room but never beat me. His neck would smell of pineapple shampoo.

## The One-legged Jockey and the Cook

Pity will not help the one-legged jockey, but will it help the pitier, who can't, however hard she tries, and cooks, not pity him?

## Cacti

On the days I pass the gate, I'll take one, although I don't always have the change. I do enjoy the succulents, of course I do, that sometimes I paid too much, sometimes too little for, but still, I would enjoy the succulents more without the constant fear they may be recognised, and carried off back home to where they came from, and that they might be cacti not succulents.

## My Mother's Bed

Across the room stood my mother's bed, piled high with eiderdowns and dressing-gowns. The light from passing cars slid round the walls. To cry or leave my cot was forbidden. All I could do was hope she wouldn't come, and hope she wouldn't kiss me, and she didn't.

## The Knife

The drawer I keep my knives in has got stuck and the knife I need to unstick it with's in the drawer.

## Timetables

Timetables, liquorice, almonds, walking backwards.

## Well-meaning Actions

The painfulness of well-meaning actions.

## Advice to the Reader

Do whatever. Hate me. I don't care. Well, that's not true. Please can I have *one*, I only need *one*, who will love me.

## My Earliest Memory

Sitting still on my father's knee. I've hated sitting still ever since, even not on someone else's knee.

## Chicken

She shouts *I'm on the phone* like a chicken shouting *Wait a sec, I'm on my nest*.

## Symptoms

'Empathy with children, animals and peasants.' She also likes snails and ants.

## All My Endless Questions

He says I can't really be interested in all the answers to all my endless questions. Yes I can. I'm getting on his nerves.

## The Orange Dress

She's just about to plunge into the waves but then she stops, goes back up the beach, folds her daughter's dress, then goes back down again to where her daughter's dipping in her toes.

## The Aunt and Her Dog

The aunt prefers new ideas to people; her dog prefers tennis balls to cake.

## Question (2)

What makes me think I'm so special anyway?

## The Lost and Found Dog Disc

She didn't give it back, she's explaining, because she didn't have their address.

## At the Pool (1)

While waiting for a shower to be free, she saves some time by putting on her clothes.

## The Visitor

I want to write and thank her for coming and say how much we all enjoyed her visit; unfortunately she is still here.

## Screams (1)

My sisters used to scream. I don't know why. Un-nerved, be-witched, I became mute.

## The Sort of Person Who

I dread the meal. I mustn't dread the meal. I mustn't be the sort of person who dreads her meals with her old friends.

## The Man Who was Crying

When I met the man who was crying, and held his hand, he couldn't stop crying.

## The Letter B

I love the letter B. I think it's funny. But no one else seems to think so too.

## A Love of Punctuation

I'm punctuating as he goes along – *well I don't know who knows we don't know do we*, for example.

## But What's It Like?

It's like being steadily sucked by something cold through a narrow slit through which there's no way home.

## Person Talking While Standing in the Sea

If you spend long enough in the water Mum it's the back of your head it gets all like O yuk I got some in my mouth I said Mum hey what are you up to now I can't hear you you wouldn't say that if O my god you can't just stand there can't see the bottom you all right there Mum she laughed her little head off.

## Her Small Son

She creeps upstairs, cradling her small son who's now a grown man and works in finance.

## Woman in a Wetsuit

The palaces, the lakes, the endless flowers; the man with the trembling lip; the stolen negligées, how do I know if they're real or if they're not?

## Snakes

Not just once, it happens all the time, and all my sister does is *complain*, so, when we reach the nettles, down she goes, I give her a good *shove* with my shoulder, and now the adults bear her away, she kicks their shins with the enormous boots they make us wear because of the snakes.

## Bereavement (1)

Bereavement is as dark as STOP is red.

## Tuesdays

She likes appointments on Tuesdays because they're blue.

## Density

When people touch me, objects change density, becoming either more or less dense and, either way, no longer being stable.

## The Library at Night

They locked me in the library by mistake and when the teacher came in in the morning she couldn't believe her eyes but I had liked it.

## Screams (2)

I used to hear my sisters scream and scream. I don't know why they screamed and screamed so much. Then one of them gave up eating sugar and the other one went to live in Africa but both of them continued to scream.

## The Girl Made of Glass

The doctor tells my parents that it's like trying to get a hold on glass and glares at me.

## Bausch

I was thinking that Isaac is an excellent name for a newt and how I wanted to call my dog Bausch but I would have had to explain who she was every time and how to spell it and I'm hypersensitive about that because of my father and my own name and the most important thing is that it sounds friendly so people are already feeling friendly towards it in the park or on the beach, for example, so when the man told me what his dog was called, I wasn't listening.

## The Telephone Call

When he rang to say his wife had died, I thought she should have told me herself.

## Hope

She'd been a bit in love with him back then, and when he gets in touch, years later, she daren't admit how full of hope she feels until the door is answered by the person who she, back then, determined not to hurt.

## The Man Who Taught Me Greek

He'd press against me like a giant cake that couldn't breathe and smelled of Number Sixes.

## The Man Shouting into His Phone

S. glares at the man shouting into his phone.
Man (shouting into his phone): Oh, nothing.

## Question (3)

So what's so clever about being clever?

## Women Carrying Bowls

While putting the blackberries straight into my mouth, I'm thinking I'm the wrong sort of woman.

## Bluebell

Bluebell was banned from the house but if she stood outside she got some cake.

## My Inability to Drive

In the same way that I can't drive, she can't believe I can't: she thinks I *won't*.

## The Same for Everyone

Maybe it's the same for everyone and everyone is thinking, deep down, everyone is thinking they're so nice why don't other people think so too?

## Somewhere in Lincolnshire

Although I much prefer the word *dovecot*, I tell myself to use the word *Boston*.

## Prayer (1)

It's true I think they're funny but it's sad to have to think they're funny by myself. Please can someone think they're funny with me.

## Her Mother's Cheek

She says her mother's cheek was *smooth* and *shiny* but why would someone slap their own mother?

## The Poodle

The poodle takes the path across the field like an aerialist across the sky.

## The Timetable

Although it was out of date, I felt grateful, but only briefly, soon I felt annoyed, but I decided not to mention it.

## The Interesting Tumble-dryer

She started to tell me about her tumble-dryer, and then I started to tell her about my neighbour's, and then she talked, with actions, about hers again, a tumble-dryer which she found more interesting.

## The Elephant Kanchenjunga

I see a spaniel wee on his head and wash him in my sister's washing-up bowl and hang him up to dry by his ears and when my sister starts to scream and shout I say to Kanchenjunga as he dries *She can shout as much as she likes, it isn't going to make the slightest difference.*

## Prayer (2)

If they approach me I think *But please don't praise me.*

## The Stolen Tennis-ball

When my dog steals the Dachshund's tennis-ball, everybody laughs except the Dachshund owner.

D.O.: That is *not* his ball!

## There's Nothing Wrong with Ducks

Four of my mugs I really don't like. But is that a reason to get rid of them? And how would I get rid of them anyway? I can't just throw them out. After all, they're perfectly nice, in their own way. One of them's from Aylesbury, for example, featuring ducks, and there's nothing wrong with ducks.

## The Widower at Night

Alone at night the widower is dreaming of dark red mouths opening and closing.

## In the Garden Shed when the Door Slams Shut

Either I curl up in tears and panic or else I go and open the door.

## The Date

Humiliated, first; then disdainful.

## The Bungalow (3)

In the cliff-top bungalow the residents cheerfully ignore each other's nakedness, sometime semi-, sometimes stark-nakedness, they cheerfully ignore it or they laugh, but either way they are in awe of it, so pure, so inexpressible, like poetry.

## Child in a Flat

As a child he used to stare at it, the patch of green below his bedroom window, the tiny people with their tiny dogs, he'd watch all day beside the Leonberger that, now he is an adult, is a real one.

## Humiliation

He used to send me down to fetch the post but, on the days I came back empty-handed, my father would be overwhelmed by something I didn't know was called *humiliation.*

## The Little Play

My mother was acting being my mother and I was acting being her child.

## Granny and the Cloud

She's lying quietly on the lawn and watching a giant penis float across the sky.

## La Belle Hélène

I don't know about her but I myself would like to have a teaspoon named after me.

## Little Things Are Happening All the Time

The room in which they find the old man appears to them as lifeless as a fridge but little things are happening all the time.

## Man in the Street

Instead of his old dog, he's with a woman he now expects to stop at every lamp-post.

## The Outing

They didn't ask her and she didn't go. The trouble is she didn't want to go. It would have been much better had she wanted to.

## Question (4)

Does she herself think she does herself, or do the others just assume she does, because it's what the others always do?

## The Dream of the Dreamer

As the dream is to reality, reality is to the written text.

## My Dog at 9 a.m.

She's waiting for me underneath my desk but I am in the garden watching ants.

## The Sound of Breaking Glass

I turned my back and walked into the sea, still fully dressed, and the man made off, and later on, maybe next day, someone came and wrapped me in a blanket and handed me, still wet, to a policeman, who promised me he wouldn't ring my mother and then I told him, which was quite true, the man who drove away was my boyfriend, he didn't think what I did was funny, he didn't really know me, I was shy, at which I think the kind policeman nodded, and then I fell asleep in his lap, and when I told the doctors what had happened my words were like the sound of breaking glass that breaks into a thousand tinkling splinters nobody can ever hope to find.

## The Surly Mothers of Successful Men (2)

The woman in the 'tummy control' swimsuit is trying to read a book of short stories while readjusting her turban, but gives up.

## The Shimmering Lake

He used to swim across it every day and then he used to walk there, but not swim; and then he walked as far as the letterbox; and then he walked round and round the room in which he was to die, in his suit.

## Mum and the Fly

Somebody had planted an oak tree beside a plaque, IN MEMORY OF MUM, but now there's nothing here except a fly.

## Ironmonger

And so, because her jeans keep slipping down, she goes into the shop to buy some string.

## September Evenings at My Grandmother's

Bluebell would be lowing in her field, Teaspoon would be mousing in the woods, my sisters would be dying in their dressing-gowns fifteen years too early of despair.

## Me-Time

The woman in the 'tummy-control' swimsuit does not want children of her own and neither does she want other people's children ruining her Sunday morning Me-Time.

## Mary (1)

I don't know why we all called him Mary, or what I was doing there, sleeping in his room, both of us were cripplingly shy, the room had nothing in it except mattresses covered with embroidered sheets and pillows, a kettle on the floor in the corner (filled up from the bathroom downstairs) and beads and sequins the mysterious girls would bring him back from London in pink bags; he used to draw huge birds on old sheets and sew along the lines with coloured wool, and sometimes we'd play jacks, and eat raisins; not a sound except the night buses; he slept all day and rarely went out; he'd sit cross-legged and sew, his waist-long hair brushed his slender knees like long minnows.

## His Other Girlfriend

When his other girlfriend stayed the night, I'd sleep on a pile of blankets on the floor. Once they had a row, and she left, and I spent the rest of the night on the bed.

## The New Cardigan

I'm sitting in my cardigan and wishing it wasn't such a lovely sunny day.

## The Most Interesting Thing About Me

Possibly the fact I was 'non-verbal', a fact that must never be mentioned.

## Heaven

In Switzerland the cows are dark red. When it's time for me to be collected, I can choose a kitten or a bear. I wait beside the lead on its hook. If I don't say *thank you* I'll be eaten. In Switzerland the snow never melts. Nor does it fall from the sky. Every child has a pet bear. For breakfast they have bowls of chocolate buttons. A second hook holds a man's hat. The Blessed Virgin Mary watches hats. In England we say *thank you* in English. In Switzerland the parents of the children *do as they are told* and make chocolate, everywhere you look there are parents stirring copper vats of roiling chocolate. 'Roiling' doesn't mean the chocolate's angry. On the contrary, it is in Heaven.

## The Prefab

He parked the van outside an old prefab and, telling me to wait till he came back, disappeared between two concrete bunkers. I found a ginger biscuit in the glove compartment and nibbled it as slowly as I could. A woman passed leading a goat then I must have fallen asleep. And it was only many years later I heard what happened on that fatal night.

## Mrs P.

I lost my key and slept in the flower-bed and in the morning Mrs P., the landlady, let me in, served me my breakfast, then stubbed her cigarette out in my egg.

## Strawberry Jam

He's taken it away from his wife because, he says, she eats it by the spoonful, so now it's me who's eating it by the spoonful.

## Who I Am

What to say but not how to say it; who I am but not how to be it.

## The Stranger's Car

He sees a stranger's car outside her house. Although he doesn't want to be her boyfriend, he certainly doesn't want to not be.

## Smoothie at Midnight

Waiting for me in the dark fridge, as patient as the lips of a horse.

## Bereavement (2)

Because you need to love someone a lot, or in a certain way she can't explain, she's trying to explain I won't, I can't, experience bereavement like she does.

## To the Reader

Yes, everything about you is beautiful, especially the fact that I don't know you.

## Fun

It would have been such fun, and it was fun, long ago, before I knew it wasn't, before I knew I had to be considerate.

## Question (5)

She says she thinks I like to be contentious but why would someone *like* to be contentious?

## As I Tried to Explain Years Later

As I tried to explain years later, I liked the doctor's rather uncaring manner.

## What I Asked the Person Standing Next to Me

I asked the person standing next to me to *squeeze me as tight as they could*, and first they looked intrigued, and then embarrassed, and then, alas, disgusted, so I left.

## China Blue

China Blue and Tuesdays, for example, go together with a sort of *click*.

## The Hearty Breakfast

After the hearty breakfast, I've decided not to go for a swim after all.

## The Blessed Virgin Mary Goes Swimming

I'm not saying I don't like the blue dress, but sometimes, instead of praying, I wonder if she'd like to try on my swimsuit.

## He Told Me To Make a List (1)

Vertigo, silver-foil, math; jazz, surprises, soft-boiled eggs; sandpaper, possessions, doctors' ears.

## The Surly Mothers of Successful Men (3)

The woman in the 'tummy control' swimsuit, having re-adjusted her turban, starts to read her book again but suddenly she chucks it in a nearby bin instead.

## Ants (2)

She's trying to talk to him but she can't. She's trying to say she loves him. *No she's not.* She's training ants to march into her bottom.

## Weight

Swimming pools, cattle, beetroot: weight. I shouted *weight*. It makes perfect sense.

## The Kitten

Each lick is like a word freed from meaning.

## Spiders

When I tuck them down inside my nightdress are they sorry I'm not more afraid?

## My Sister's Hair

It may be clean but it's much too thin.

## Cucumber

Not because I like it but because I don't dislike it.

## He Told Me To Make a List (2)

Garage forecourts, rubber bands, sieves; emery boards, meat, the smell of privet.

## Prayer (3)

The stockings on her legs are too dry. *Please can I have another, moister grandmother.*

## The Problems of Taking It in Turns

Chatting, say, or choosing fairy cakes.

## At the Pool (2)

I'm standing with a towel round my head because I don't like crowds but I do like towels.

## The Irish Terrier and the Irish Terrier's Owner

S.: Oh he's so nice, I love him!
I.T.O.: He loves you as well, it's just he's a bit wary...
S.: I would be wary too if I loved me as well.

## Thicket

The doctor calls it living without a brake. Or living without a Kit-Kat, or a thicket.

## On Passing a Field with 7 Cows and 7 Sheep in It

Exactly seven cows and seven sheep and God is in His Heaven doing maths.

## The Bungalow (4)

Far too late the waves unroll and glitter, ices drip, unruly seagulls scream, it's far too late and noisy for the residents, who go to sleep in the afternoon.

## Yes

*Yes*, I said, *I'm fine*, but I wasn't.

## Two Cows in a Meadow

An orange cow is standing in a meadow innocently smelling some flowers when her sister comes along and *butts* her because her sister's getting on her nerves.

## You and Me

It's not because *I am me*, exactly, but because *you are not me*.

## The Clinical Psychologist (1)

How sad, to think I don't know what to do; how sad to be so earnest, and so wrong.

## My Friends

Not only the things they don't, the things they do, do: they don't avoid hugging; they eat fish.

## The Surprise Birthday Present

While she eats the chocolate, she is crying: the chocolate is good, but *it's not a puppy*.

## My Grandmother's Dressing-gown

The doctor blinks and whispers he is sorry and as he blinks my grandmother grows wings, they're sprouting through her sky-blue towelling dressing-gown, soft and downy, hardening into quills.

## Zvuv

My sister's like the Yiddish word for gnat – she's small, she's vicious and she can't stop whining.

## The Clinical Psychologist (2)

He's peering at me like an Englishman peering at a Finn or a Norwegian and congratulating himself on spelling fjord.

## B. on Honeymoon

He finds himself in a different world, a world in which he'll always be a stranger.

## A & E

That woman who I sat with in the waiting-room, blood and vomit everywhere, was me.

## Things She Wishes She Had Brought on Holiday

Vegan dog biscuits, a clothes-airer, a pair of proper beach shoes, some cheesecake, a cleaner washing-up bowl, a paddle-board, a poncho, pine kernels, tweezers, bananas and a pop-up tent for the children.

## Clairvoyance

The woman in the 'tummy control' swimsuit has waited three months for this appointment and now she doesn't know if she can face it, she doesn't even know if she can spell it.

## My Dentist's Eyes

My dentist's eyes are like the blue sky shining through two holes in his skull.

## The Search

She looked for him all day but never found him.

## The General's Pyjamas

Now that the general's fence has been blown down, the general's large, immaculate pyjamas are clearly visible on his washing-line.

## My Sister Whines

My sister whines like one of Hayling Island's famously bloodthirsty mosquitos.

## Purity of Heart

Can the mother's purity of heart withstand the father's unrelenting pessimism?

## Wasps (1)

They stacked the empty jars behind the gym, and that's where you could find me, on hot days, smeared with jam and quivering with wasps.

## The Barista

She asks him where he's sitting, but he's standing.

## The Woman with Thick Ankles

When I see a woman with thick ankles, I think to myself *She was young once.*

## The Level Crossing

I took the train each morning and each morning I used to feel sorry for the people who lived beside the railway-line, because the level crossing was never open.

## As the Bus Sails Past My Stop

As the bus sails past my stop, I find myself thinking to myself *Where's the person who normally rings the bell*; and then remember, but too late, she's me.

## My First Giraffe

At first I took her out on a string but very soon I'd trained her to follow me, and answer to her name, which was Topsy. She was an albino, all white, which is very rare for a giraffe. She met an early death on Christmas Eve when Father Christmas accidentally trod on her.

## Father (2)

If he met his cleaner on the stairs he'd tell her it was time to go home because he couldn't bear to hear the sound her brush made knocking on the banisters and newel posts.

## My Own Mother

If I'm fascinated by my brain, it means I'm fascinated by myself but being fascinated by myself is *not allowed*; or by anything: it frightens people if you're too intense, the way, he says, I frightened my own mother.

## A Simple Question

Sometimes when I'm asked a simple question I hear the sound but what it means escapes me, the way exotic snakes escape vivaria.

## The Woman in the Drawing-room

I couldn't understand, as a child, why she was in bed *in the drawing-room* or why she didn't speak, or have a husband, or why her mouth was such a peculiar shape, or who the man who was a vicar was, or why, when I was scared, he said *I told you so*.

## Mary (2)

He brought a bag of cake and broken biscuits, we couldn't understand a word he said, except the word *babe*, he kept repeating it, he peered into the room with a smile, and Mary smiled but didn't let him in, I heard him creeping back into his room, it was Christmas, Mary shut the door, and the three mysterious girls continued smoking.

## What to Say

It's not as if I don't know what to say; I do know what to say, of course I do; it's waiting, what to say, like a coin – what to say but not how to say it.

## Apricot Lover

The apricot is almost six foot high. My arms and legs hang down the sides like cream. I'm lying on the top, on my stomach, the letters of *velociraptor* watching me.

## My Mother in Particular

My mother, in particular, was puzzling. She seemed to be disappointed in me.

## Herons

The herons pass slowly overhead like glasses of cold water that can fly.

## Wasps (2)

As I got bolder and more bored, I also smeared the jam on my nipples.

## The Clinical Psychologist (3)

Although he thinks I don't understand, I do, I do, it makes perfect sense.

## Pins

While the doctors ask me all their questions, their heads are shrinking to the size of pins.

## The Child Within

Not 'the child within' so much as the adult without.

## The Man Who Walks 30 Miles a Day

He says there was a beautiful young lady to whom he was abusive and he's walking in order to atone for his sins.

## Lambs

On Saturdays we walked to the tobacconist's where I bought me, first, a chocolate penny and, secondly, a pack of woolly pipe-cleaners. I put the chocolate penny in my wallet, the pipe-cleaners I made into lambs.

## Cow at Night

I hear her heavy breath below my window, she breathes for me, she breathes for the owl, she breathes for all the crushed and blameless beetles she's much too big to be aware of crushing.

## The Birthday Present

He gave me seven apricots in syrup and as we sat and reminisced he ate them.

## Ice Hockey

Stationed on the ice, completely naked, I haven't got a clue what's going on.

## Question (7)

So one of us is 'refusing to make allowances', but is it me or is it the psychologist?

## The Bishop Digs a Hole

The bishop digs the hole nice and deep in order to fit everything in and afterwards he runs the hottest bath it's ever been his privilege to wallow in.

## Sideboard

Apricots, a Bible and a snowman. From time to time the snowman climbs down and goes to see the apricots, who blank him.

## The Bungalow (5)

Everyone's falling asleep, sleeping for the simple love of sleeping, of being not yet dead but asleep.

## The Peacock

Little did I know that one fine day admiring his topiary peacock would seem quite normal.

## Birds

Warrot, weahen, wover, wheasant, widgeon.

## The Loving Hand

Ever since the day I had the row, I can't remember even who with, and set off on my bicycle in tears, and found myself sobbing at the piggery where men in yellow boiler-suits with buckets were whacking giant sows on their haunches, men I was afraid of being seen with, miles from the village as we were, nothing but ploughed fields in all directions, flocks of plovers, hares, but no people, ever since she stood in my way and let me scratch her bristly ear, and grunted, I grunt like her, not out loud, obviously, I grunt like her, the sow, as if I too can feel someone scratching my ear, someone or something, a hand, lovingly scratching my ear.

## Happy Birthday

Rhubarb pickle that they've made themselves, a photograph of Federer 'in action', a book of short stories called *The Bungalow* and a Christmas card from the ex-pool attendant.

## The Parrot

I was thinking I felt like a parrot with four legs when I actually felt like a parrot with three legs.

## Golf

You know the man I met, I think I told you, who called me *chic* that time (I think by *chic* he only meant I didn't have the jumper on that made him say I looked like a *teapot*), this man, I found out yesterday, *plays golf*, but just because I know he plays golf it doesn't mean to say I can't talk to him, and maybe it's, for him, the first time he's spoken to a person who *hates golf*, and maybe that's exactly why he talks to me, he needs me *to save him from golf*, together we will liberate the fairways, where animals that no one's seen before, animals with eyes like monks', will roam and men in handmade jumpers will be seen flopped on handmade blankets eating buns.

## Omelette

The widower knows seven charming widows, one of whom owns a hen called Omelette, who likes to lay her eggs in the drawing-room, in the broken basket of kindling behind the sofa.

## The Right Amount of Smiling

She'll need some help with the right amount of smiling.

## The Man Who Doesn't Want To Be Forgiven

He doesn't want to be forgiven anyway, not because there's nothing to forgive but because forgiveness is too 'intimate'.

## The Happy Couple

The very old couple holding hands are said to be brother and sister.

## My Sister Accuses Me of Being an Attention-seeker

And does the deer 'seek' the tick's attention?

## Faith

When is praying chanting and chanting singing, does a mother always love her child, what does *being intimate* actually mean, what's the point of being *careful* anyway, could his older sister be his mother, why do millipedes have so many legs, why is she so upset but I'm not, is it true all I need is *faith*, does the daddy-long-legs feel the cold, why can't I grow fur and swim with dogs?

## Mayonnaise

The upstairs room they have confined me in is overrun by triangles on legs, they swarm across the carpet, climb the furniture, and gather in white drifts on the bed; one of them starts creeping up my neck, I whisper *Would you like some mayonnaise* (nothing, I've been told, annoys them more) and, sure enough, the triangle takes off, flying through the air like a bird while tucking up its tiny white bootees.

## The Spoon (Testing My Powers of Observation)

My father used to send me outside, rearrange something, like a spoon, maybe only move it by an inch, then call me back and sit and watch me work and, in this way, my hands behind my back, I first became aware of my existence.

## The Cold Fish

Because I'm different, because I think I'm different but I'm not, because I'm not different, because I think I'm so clever, because I'm a serial killer and push little children off balconies, because I can't be trusted, because I'm a cold fish, because I get on everybody's nerves, because I'm just making excuses, because I don't want to even think about it, because I just want to be loved like everybody else, because I don't, as soon as he puts the kettle on, I run for it.

## Cookie

Someone I can't see is approaching me so close I feel their breath on my neck, they lean against me in the dark and tell me what the Dutch for cookie is, and laugh, because they're you, the reader I keep dreaming of.

## The Burning House

He's shattering the glass with his fist, leaping in, dragging her away, the child who will spend her life re-living the joy of being taken in his arms.

## The Bungalow (6)

On the beach below, the children laugh, darting here and there like little birds, while in the garden of the cliff-top bungalow the residents have gone back to sleep.

# [NOTES]

# NOTES

## Self-portrait with a Bucket

I dedicate the cardboard skirt to Harriet, the swimming pool to the Whistling Man, the word 'albeit' to Phoebe, the hornet to Archie and the octopi to Julia Copus. (Did you know that their tentacles can climb out of buckets even after their heads have been chopped off?) I dedicate the sand to John and Victoria Mitchell and the 'curly-headed women can't kick' quote to X. (He knows who he is.)

## Room 17

***The Grandmother's Sofa:*** The choreographer Pina Bausch has talked about how she believes in her dancers' commitment to overcoming the limits of their fragility with discipline.

***The Grandmother and the Rat:*** In 2023, seventy-one children starved to death in an orphanage in Ukraine.

***The Grandmother at the Grand Hotel:*** Why walk when you can totter?

# ACKNOWLEDGEMENTS

Thanks are due to Nadia Kingsley and Fairacre Press who published pamphlet editions of *Men in Shorts* (2022) and *Baby Peter* (with photographs by Maisie Hill, 2024).

**EU DECLARATION OF GPSR CONFORMITY**